AWAKENING THE
SLEEPING BUDDHA

AWAKENING THE SLEEPING BUDDHA

The Twelfth
TAI SITUPA

Edited by Lea Terhune

SHAMBHALA
Boston & London

Shambhala Publications, Inc.
Horticultural Hall
300 Massachusetts Avenue
Boston, MA 02115

9 8 7 6 5 4 3 2 1

First Edition

Printed in the United States of America

Distributed in the United States by Random House, Inc.,
and in Canada by Random House of Canada Ltd

Library of Congress Cataloging-in-Publication Data

Pema Donyo Nyinche, Tai Situpa XII, 1954–
Awakening the sleeping Buddha/The Twelfth Tai Situpa; edited by
Lea Terhune.—1st ed.
p.   cm.
ISBN 1-57062-185-3 (alk. paper)
1. Buddhism—Doctrines.   I. Terhune, Lea.   II. Title.
BQ4132.P47   1996   96-16429
294.3'42—dc20   CIP

— CONTENTS —

——INTRODUCTION——

BUDDHISM CAN APPEAR so complicated and vast that it seems even a lifetime of study would not be sufficient to get to the bottom of it. That is how it is, from one perspective—at least until the ultimate goal of enlightenment is reached. On the other hand, Buddhism can be very simple, dissolving mysteries and complications easily with common-sense truths. Buddhism, in fact, encompasses both these extremes, although the foundation of Buddhist philosophy and practice rests on a few clear principles.

A number of core ideas occur again and again, and gaining an understanding of these is perhaps the most important accomplishment for anyone who wishes to study and apply Buddhist tenets in his or her life. A grasp of these essential principles provides firm ground that will be the foundation of limitless progress later, whatever level of Buddhist study is undertaken. This book is an attempt to clarify a few of the topics that come up most often in teachings and discussions of Mahayana Buddhist thought.

We begin at the beginning with buddha nature, because that is the most important concept to understand. Then, for the Mahayanist, comes bodhichitta. How the recognition of buddha nature is accomplished and the field in which we learn to practice bodhichitta is dealt with in a discussion of reincarnation and karma. Understanding emptiness brings us into a position to study Tantric science, of which the Mahamudra is an example of the highest form. It is through the practice of such Tantric sciences that we gain realization through the transformation they precipitate.

As the process of transformation moves forward, realization can come at any time or in any place. Realization itself has many aspects, leading to the highest realization that transcends subject and object, relative and absolute—all samsaric manifestations. Every moment of life, and the intermediate states between life and death and between sleeping and waking, are the means of attaining realization. Every mistake and every success leads gradually to the ultimate goal. The ultimate goal of Buddhist study and practice is, of course, the state of being completely purified, the enlightenment of a buddha.

AWAKENING THE
SLEEPING BUDDHA

—— *ONE* ——
BUDDHA NATURE

THE FOUNDATION OF LORD BUDDHA'S TEACH-
ing is buddha nature. It is because of buddha nature that
the Buddha taught at all. Every sentient being has the potential
to improve and become enlightened. We can improve and overcome any defilements we have because of buddha nature, which
is our pure and enlightened essential nature. The Buddha shared
his insights about this not only to acknowledge the fact of buddha nature within every sentient being, but to guide individuals
to awaken this innate and limitless potential to the point where
they fully realize their own buddha nature and become enlightened buddhas themselves.

It is important to understand that buddha nature is not something we imagine or create from nothing. It is something that
exists within each sentient being already, and the gradual
method the Buddha taught is designed to awaken the ever-
present buddha nature by instructing individuals at different levels of development exactly how to do this.

Although we all have buddha nature as our ultimate reality,
in our ordinary reality, which might be called our relative world,
there are many differences between individuals. For this reason
the Buddha taught in different ways. Later, his teachings were
divided into four main categories, the Vinaya, Abhidharma, Sutras, and Tantras. Each category integrates all the teachings,
placing emphasis on a particular area. The Vinaya teachings
deal primarily with discipline and present a moral code; Abhidharma is mainly concerned with science, the fine details of how

Essence of buddha nature

the universe is formed and the laws that operate in it; the Sutras focus on teachings about compassion; and the Tantras present the methods of transformation by which gradual realization and finally enlightenment can be accomplished. The purpose of these teachings is simply to assist individuals to awaken their ultimate essence, their buddha nature.

Lord Buddha introduced the concept of buddha nature when he gave the Mahayana teachings, particularly in texts such as the *Lotus Sutra, Lankavatara-sutra,* and *Dasa Bhumi-sutra.* In his first teaching, the Buddha presented the Four Noble Truths. These truths are: life is pervaded by suffering; suffering has causes; there is a goal, because the causes of suffering can be destroyed; and there is a path, because a method exists to root out the causes of suffering. The Buddha explained that through discipline, mindfulness, and right actions we develop calmness and clearness. The final development of calmness and clearness is freedom from all things that obscure the clear, fresh nature within. This allows a deep and abiding inner peace. What remains when the defilements leave is buddha nature, the essence of which is peace. Even in the Four Noble Truths, the Buddha's first teaching, he expressed the principle of buddha nature.

In the Tantric teachings of the Buddha, buddha nature is the foundation, the path, and the fruition. Buddha nature is described as being ultimately unstained by any defilement. It is just like space, which cannot ultimately be stained by anything. Even the being who is suffering in hell has a pure buddha nature.

An important Mahayana teaching in which buddha nature is discussed in some detail is the *Mahayana-uttara-tantra,* one of the teachings of Lord Maitreya, which was transmitted to the great master Asanga. Lord Maitreya is a great bodhisattva who is not in human form, although he is able to teach human beings who are advanced enough to understand the level on which he teaches. Asanga was able to bring these teachings to the human realm. Maitreya's teachings are a sound introduction to the subject of buddha nature.

Lord Maitreya gave five teachings to Asanga, of which the *Mahayana-uttara-tantra* was the last. He specifically emphasized that his teachings were not those of a buddha, but a commentary on the teachings of the Buddha. *Uttara-tantra* has two meanings. It is *uttara* because it is the highest of the five teachings given by Lord Maitreya to his disciple Asanga, and it is the fifth and last teaching.

LORD MAITREYA'S EXPLICATION OF BUDDHA NATURE

In the teaching given to Asanga, Lord Maitreya provides comprehensive information about buddha nature under four headings. These are important to study and understand:

- The buddha nature of all sentient beings
- Qualities of buddha nature
- Obstacles that prevent sentient beings from recognizing buddha nature, and the means to overcome the obstacles
- Disadvantages of not knowing and benefits of knowing about buddha nature

ALL SENTIENT BEINGS HAVE BUDDHA NATURE

Sentient beings have buddha nature, whether they know about it or not. They may be totally ignorant of buddha nature, may have some awareness of it, or may be completely awakened, but in all three stages of development, sentient beings have buddha nature.

When a sentient being is ignorant of buddha nature, its essence is nevertheless ever present, as in a fertile seed, always ready to germinate. When a sentient being develops, buddha nature manifests as knowledge, wisdom, good thoughts, and good actions. When a sentient being attains enlightenment, enlightenment itself is buddha nature. The individual realizes his or her buddha nature completely—that is enlightenment.

It is on the ultimate level that every sentient being is buddha. There is no difference between the ultimate nature of an ignorant sentient being and the enlightened buddha. The essence is ultimately the same. The only difference is that the sentient being is ignorant of this, and a buddha completely embodies it. The sentient being is relatively unenlightened, and innately buddha, while a buddha is both relatively and ultimately enlightened. A buddha is, in fact, beyond relative and ultimate, which are dualistic designations.

Lord Maitreya explains that every sentient being has the potential for enlightenment. There is no sentient being who cannot improve and become enlightened eventually. This is so because every sentient being has buddha nature, regardless of which realm that sentient being belongs to. Every sentient being is ultimately perfect. Relatively, because of what are called, in Buddhism, defilements, sentient beings have countless imperfections. Defilements are things like anger, pride, and grasping. The purpose of Dharma practice is to apply the most effective method to overcome those imperfections. With the right method, a person can gradually awaken and overcome all defilements that prevent recognition of inner truth and realization of buddha nature.

Lord Maitreya said that as far as the ultimate potential of a being is concerned, there is no difference between one who is a fully enlightened buddha and one who is totally ignorant. Such a statement might be confusing without a clear understanding of the nature of truth. Truth has two aspects: relative, or changeable truth, and ultimate, changeless truth. It is on the relative level that the obstacles arise. The ultimate level is pure. It is buddha nature. On the relative level we are not yet buddhas, but on the ultimate level we are. On the relative level we encounter all sorts of problems; on the ultimate level there are no problems. Our understanding of the actual nature of truth must be through this contrast.

A good thing to remember is that there is a direct connection between the ultimate and the relative. The ultimate is the ultimate of the relative and the relative is the relative of the ultimate. They are not two different things. So when Lord Maitreya says that no matter how ordinary or negative a person might appear to be, that person has no limitation as far as his or her deeper essence is concerned, he is speaking about the relative and ultimate aspects of truth. Ultimately, there is no difference between sentient beings who are suffering in samsara and a buddha who is completely enlightened and free from all limitations. They are the same. It is good to contemplate this paradox.

QUALITIES OF BUDDHA NATURE

Lord Maitreya goes on to explain that buddha nature is limitless. It is beyond time, beyond size, beyond quality, beyond any limitation at all. Ultimately there is no limitation, but relatively, there is limitation, as an individual strives toward greater awakening.

Lord Maitreya states that buddha nature is utterly pure. It cannot be obscured itself, although relative perception of it can be obscured. Every sentient being is ready to be enlightened at every moment. The only hindrance is not recognizing the purity and limitlessness of buddha nature. We may have inklings of our limitless quality, but we don't fully recognize it, so we become focused on the relative I, the self. Every moment we are enlightened, but we don't recognize it. So every moment we are prevented from recognizing this, we cannot be fully enlightened. This sort of dualism creates all dualistic causes and conditions, which manifest as bad and good, light and dark, positive and negative. It is like a long dream.

To wake up from the dualistic dream, one must make certain

efforts, which include right behavior, calming the mind through meditation, and other techniques that develop insight and realization. Individual practice takes many forms. It can be meditation or it can be action. The point is to improve our perceptions, experience, and expression of our own buddha nature. It is easy, however, to become attracted to something negative and become more ignorant and deluded as a result. Lord Maitreya said that until you reach the stage of first-level bodhisattva, you can improve or you can become deluded. After achieving the first-level bodhisattva stage, you cannot become deluded. Even though buddha nature is limitless, relatively it can be obscure.

FOUR PRINCIPLES OF PURIFICATION

The *Mahayana-uttara-tantra shastra* says that we must first develop a clear understanding that will allow us to respect and appreciate the right things, those things that benefit ourselves and others. Once we have that, the next step is to know how to practice, that is, how to go about our development. We need to know what is right, but we must also know the proper method of applying and expanding our understanding so that we do not go wrong. The third principle is the development of loving-kindness and compassion. Loving-kindness and compassion will allow our understanding and appreciation to be progressively more successful. If we don't have loving-kindness and compassion, our progress will stop. We may even become proud of ourselves and regress. We develop loving-kindness and compassion so that we will proceed forward rather than go backward.

The stages of development are described as stages of purification. We purify our defilements, and then we reach a higher level of realization. What is there to be purified? The defilements that obscure the reality of our buddha nature, ultimately already pure, are what must be purified. Ultimately there is nothing to purify. Relatively, we must purify the obscurations to realize the underlying purity.

The means for purification are many, and Lord Maitreya gives specific suggestions. To overcome ignorance, he advises strong aspiration. It can be a simple thing, as simple as the desire to do what is right, or do one's best. Even if we don't know how to go about it, if we have the aspiration, we will begin to discover the way to fulfill it. A result of aspiration is a gradual development of wisdom, wisdom that enables one to see clearly what is right, what is appropriate, and what is essential. When wisdom is developed, profound compassion and devotion follow naturally. Lord Maitreya goes on to say that because of profound devotion and profound compassion, which are the products of wisdom, and which are in turn the product of aspiration, realization will take place.

If a sentient being misunderstands the truth and thereby moves farther and farther away from correct understanding, that sentient being is also far from recognizing his or her buddha nature. Methods are described in Asanga's text that create the causes and conditions for purification, which brings individuals closer to the correct view. These are given by Lord Maitreya in the form of four principles.

After cultivation of loving-kindness and compassion, Lord Maitreya described a fourth means of purification. He advised contemplation to transcend fear and greed.

GRADUAL FRUITION

After describing the condition of purification in four stages, Lord Maitreya describes the different levels of fruition, or the results of the application of the means of purification. He says that fruition simply means awakening of the ultimate essence, stressing the gradual process of realization. The awakening of a person's buddha nature, from the beginning to enlightenment, takes many lifetimes. According to Lord Maitreya, each stage of awakening, each moment, is a fruition of the previous moment. He gives an elaborate description of this.

He says that first we have to be able to acknowledge that we have defilements, we have negativity, we make mistakes. We have to be able to accept this instead of deluding ourselves that we don't make mistakes, that our actions are perfect or even almost perfect. We have to be able to accept that we're sometimes neurotic.

Once we know we have defilements, we can apply methods to overcome them. At the same time, we must know that ultimately we are perfect, ultimately we are not negative, ultimately we don't have defilements. This understanding will help us in overcoming the defilements and negativity.

We should realize the same thing about other sentient beings. We have to be able to see that these sentient beings are suffering. It is not only we ourselves who are suffering, but all sentient beings. And we have to do something to help them whenever it's appropriate. We pray, "May I be able to do something for them." We must wish to be able to help other sentient beings. That has to happen first. While we apply effort to overcoming the suffering of others, to helping them, we also must recognize that all these sentient beings have buddha nature. Ultimately they are not neurotic or stupid, but perfect. All this suffering and neurosis is just relative truth. We must be able to see that.

These are the fruitions we reach in each stage. Then we gradually proceed toward becoming a bodhisattva. What is a bodhisattva? A bodhisattva is an individual who has gone beyond the ordinary sort of activity, and whose realization is so advanced that his or her actions are always purely motivated and positive. We progress through the levels of bodhisattva attainment, from the first to the tenth, until finally we become completely enlightened, a buddha. These are the stages of the awakening of our buddha nature.

THE FOUR WHEELS

Lord Maitreya explains some key methods for progressing along the path toward realization. These methods are known as the four wheels, because a wheel can take us from one place to another. These particular four wheels will take us from samsara to enlightenment.

The first wheel is guidance. We should follow proper guidance. If we don't have correct guidance, even if we have sincere aspiration, we have only our own judgment to rely on, and due to our ignorance, anxiety, and ego, that judgment can often be faulty. So accurate and truthful guidance is necessary.

Tibetan Buddhism strictly holds that everything we learn or teach should be the continuation of a lineage of transmission. A lineage of transmission, in Buddhist terms, may be explained simply. Lord Buddha's teaching is a teaching based on realization. Buddha's teaching came about as a spontaneous manifestation of this realization, and therefore it is a teaching of enlightenment, which comes from completely enlightened body, speech, and mind. It is an expression of compassion and wisdom. That is the beginning of the lineage.

Buddha taught spontaneously to his disciples. They practiced the method he taught them, and in turn they taught it to their disciples. Every teaching we pass on in Tibetan Buddhism is the continuation of the practice of the original teaching the Buddha taught, which his disciples practiced and passed on to their disciples, and so on. That is the lineage of transmission. It is also the source of correct guidance.

The teacher practices the teachings and shares them with whomever comes to receive teachings. This is done carefully, however. In the past, teachers put disciples through many tests before passing on the advanced teachings to be sure the teaching would help rather than harm the individual. A genuine teacher-disciple relationship is not something taken lightly. It is a commitment for both the teacher and the student.

The second wheel is living our lives according to the principles of Buddhist Dharma. When we practice Dharma, it is important to live a dharmic life. We should not practice diligently for a few hours and then run wild the rest of the day, leaving our calm and clear state of mind behind on the meditation cushion. When we meditate or chant mantras or do any kind of practice, we should take it seriously not only during the formal practice period, but outside of it as well. It should extend into all the activities of our daily life. We should live as closely to the teachings as possible. We might make mistakes—that is normal—but we do the best we can to live according to the teachings and to remain as centered in our daily activities as we are when doing formal meditation. In Vajrayana, everything becomes meditation. Everything is a source of realization. It can only really become so, though, when the mind is clear and calm at all times.

The third wheel is virtuous conduct. Intensive meditation can be a deep level of virtue. The external aspect of virtue is doing helpful things for others. It is very important for Buddhists to perform activities that are helpful for other people. We should not only develop the mind, we must also be aware of the needs of others and ways we might help fill these needs. Sometimes one small positive action on the part of an individual can have a great positive effect on others. Virtuous conduct can be anything from saving the lives of beings, giving direct aid to those who are suffering, or merely offering a kind word at the right time. This sort of activity should be practiced as much as possible.

The fourth wheel is profound aspiration toward enlightenment. This is very important to maintain, because it keeps us

going through the worst difficulties. There is nothing wrong
with ambitious aspiration to become enlightened. It should be a
sincere and deep desire not only to attain enlightenment oneself,
but for other sentient beings likewise to attain it. Lord Maitreya
says the same thing that we find in the main Buddhist prayers:
"May all sentient beings attain total liberation." When we look
at our planet, or even at a single country, we see how much
work there is to be done. People cannot even get along with each
other in the same city. The prospect of enlightenment appears
far away and unimaginable. How can we sincerely mean it when
we pray that all sentient beings attain enlightenment? How can
we think it is even possible? But it is possible. It is possible because every sentient being has buddha nature.

THE FULFILLMENT OF BUDDHA NATURE

Next, Lord Maitreya explains that the fulfillment and goal of
our pure, perfect, and limitless buddha nature is enlightenment.
All sentient beings, having buddha nature, will attain enlightenment ultimately. It may take some sentient beings a long time to
purify their defilements and recognize their buddha nature, but
others may become enlightened more quickly. It is based on how
the individual being pursues the path to realization, and what
choices are made. One thing is certain: all beings will be able to
do this because their essence is buddha.

Lord Maitreya goes on to say that ignorant sentient beings
are unaware of their buddha nature because of the dualistic aspect of their minds. The dualistic mind of a sentient being does
not recognize the essence of his or her nature. Some degree of
buddha nature is recognized in the dualistic mind of a bodhisattva or a developed individual. When a person becomes buddha, the dualistic aspect of mind is totally purified. Mind is
beyond dualism. The fully awakened person becomes the embodiment of buddha nature, transcending all limitations. For

that reason, a buddha's activity is limitless. A bodhisattva's activity is limited compared to a buddha's activity, and an ordinary sentient being's activity is extremely limited.

QUALITIES AND CHARACTERISTICS OF BUDDHA NATURE

Lord Maitreya elaborates on the characteristics of buddha nature. He says that buddha nature is unchangeable. No matter how ignorant we are, our buddha nature remains the same. No matter how enlightened we are, our buddha nature remains the same. It is the changeless nature. Enlightenment is the full embodiment of our buddha nature in all levels of our manifestation as sentient beings. All the qualities of the Buddha, such as the ten great strengths, and all the ways we describe and define the qualities of a buddha—these are all qualities of the buddha nature.

When we attain enlightenment, we realize the full extent of these qualities. The activity of a buddha is beyond dualism. In one sutra Lord Buddha said, "I never taught anything." What this implies is that all teachings passed down from Lord Buddha were spontaneous manifestations. It is not simply one person talking to another person. Spontaneous manifestation is like the shining of the sun, and it carries with it the real power to aid individual development. Sunlight does so many things. It warms the seed so the seed can develop into a shoot and take root in soil. Sunlight ripens fruit on the trees. It gives light. It warms the oceans, and the steam rises and forms clouds. All this is spontaneous manifestation, without a conceptual plan, just as a buddha's activity is spontaneous.

Because a buddha's activity is nondualistic, a buddha can aid others. The Buddha, who has transcended duality, is limitless, so that even if the whole universe recites the refuge prayer and asks for blessings at the same time, the Buddha's blessing will be given equally, according to each individual's capacity to receive it.

OVERCOMING THE OBSCURATIONS

When Lord Maitreya discusses obstacles and how to overcome them, he speaks of "temporary obscurations." There is no such thing as a permanent obscuration. Obscurations are always temporary. Lord Maitreya said there were endless obscurations, but he defined nine major ones: attachment, anger, ignorance, and six types of obstacles that concern bodhisattvas between the first and tenth levels.

The first obstacle that prevents an individual from recognizing buddha nature is attachment. Attachment is a very powerful obscuration, and it strongly reinforces dualistic thinking. Attachment simply means we are attached to the cycle of existence, or samsara. Lord Maitreya said that through methods of transformation, we must find a way to establish balance so that our attachment becomes first a reasonable attachment, rather than an unreasonable one. Then we slowly overcome that attachment and become not detached, but purely nonattached. Freedom from attachment must be developed.

One of the means for overcoming attachment, according to the text, is a clear and accurate understanding of the relative truth of everything. Lord Maitreya says that one truth about all existence is impermanence. Wherever we go in this world, we always find ruins of temples, palaces, houses, and other structures that were once new and in daily use, perhaps for centuries. People once worked hard to build these places and spent a lot of money on them, but now the buildings are no more than interesting historical monuments, or maybe not even that.

When we develop accurate understanding, we might still be involved in samsaric activities, such as building houses, careers, or relationships, but we won't be attached to them unreasonably and neurotically. We will understand that these things are not permanent. They have no ultimate value, but only relative value, because they exist interdependently and are always changing. That is an important first step, and it helps us avoid easily falling prey to negative thoughts and actions.

If we don't have clear understanding, we will become jealous if somebody builds a house that is bigger than ours. That may seem ridiculous, but it happens. One temple congregation will try to stop the other temple from developing, saying, "My Buddha is better than your Buddha." All these things can happen because of attachment, combined with other negative factors.

Then Lord Maitreya taught about anger and aggression. He said that anger is powerful, although it is not as constant as attachment. It comes and goes. Attachment is continuous, especially in the human realm, which is described as the desire realm or the realm of attachment. Anger normally develops out of some disturbance that obstructs the fulfillment of our desires. We are attached to something, and something interferes with our having it, so we get angry, and sometimes we even become aggressive in our efforts to get what we want. One of the main methods for overcoming anger is to develop understanding of other people's suffering and defilements, and to have compassion for others.

Ignorance is one of the roots of obscuration, like desire, anger, and aggression. Ignorance is the result of not seeing things deeply, as they actually are, but merely seeing the surface. Most of the time we don't even see the surface accurately. In some of the Vajrayana practice instructions, great masters have written that most human beings totally misunderstand each other. They function with 100 percent misunderstanding. Even good practitioners, who are very learned and highly disciplined, can be affected by external circumstances from which attachment or anger can develop. It may not be obvious, but it is there at an unconscious level, ready to come up under appropriate stimuli. Until the attainment of the first-level bodhisattva, ignorance is present.

The fourth obscuration, karma, is the result of the combination of attachment, aggression, and ignorance. Karma, which is a Sanskrit word, is in such common usage that it appears in English dictionaries. Even so, not many people know precisely what it means, and they often misunderstand it. If their businesses are failing or marriages breaking up, people might ask, "Is it my bad karma?" According to the teaching of the Buddha, karma means causes and conditions. Of course, there are causes and conditions that create failures in business or marriage and other difficulties, so people assume "It's karma." The unfortunate thing about this is that an idea becomes fixed in the mind that if it is karma, we are helpless; it is a fate that cannot be changed. That idea is wrong, because it is absolutely untrue. Bad karma can be improved and become good karma, and good karma can be destroyed and become bad karma. More will be said about karma later. Karma does not exist as an entity. Karma is a word that describes the relative causes and conditions that create our lives.

Lord Maitreya described the fifth obscuration as "unconscious dualistic states of mind" (Tib. *palcha*). These are states that are dormant in the mind but that can manifest under certain circumstances and stimuli. It is like a sleeping monster if it is a negative state, or a sleeping angel if it is positive. It is almost like instinct. It is an unconscious habit we carry with us from lifetime to lifetime.

The next obstacle prevents recognition of buddha nature, that is, from becoming a first-level bodhisattva. We become a first-level bodhisattva when we realize our buddha nature and the true essence of everything for the first time. All the practice methods of a bodhisattva are aimed at overcoming the obscurations that prevent the individual from recognizing buddha nature. The state of recognizing buddha nature is the realization of the first-level bodhisattva.

The succeeding series of obscurations described by Maitreya refers to higher and higher levels of bodhisattva attainment. These are increasingly subtle dualistic obstacles that are overcome by the practice of bodhisattvas at those stages. This is a point where even the higher levels of wisdom and intellectual understanding become hindrances and must be purified. In the case of the seventh obscuration, for instance, it is the bodhisattva's realization of buddha nature that must be overcome.

When speaking about levels of bodhisattva realization, obviously we can explore it only theoretically. To understand exactly what a first-level bodhisattva is, one must be one. If an ordinary person were to be confronted with a buddha and a first-level bodhisattva together, telling them apart would not be so easy. It would be easy to confuse them, because from our dualistic level, there is no way of discerning the difference. On their level, however, a first-level bodhisattva and a buddha are quite different, but the distinctions are at a level too subtle for ordinary minds to recognize.

An ordinary person has meditative and nonmeditative states. But to an ordinary person, the nonmeditative state of a first-level bodhisattva is like realization, for a bodhisattva of the first level or beyond has transcended the difference between meditative and nonmeditative states. It is more accurate to speak of a postmeditative state, because the meditative state permeates the activity of a bodhisattva, even when the bodhisattva is not engaged in formal meditation practice. At this level of development there is nothing that is not understood or recognized. The bodhisattva's accomplishment is not intellectual; it is direct realization. The bodhisattva overcomes the difference between meditative and nonmeditative states, so that both become equal. Of course, to a second-level bodhisattva the accomplishments of a first-level bodhisattva are limited. A bodhisattva of a higher level of realization can perceive faults in the states of mind of bodhisattvas of lower levels. That is only natural. Until complete enlightenment, there is always room for improvement.

Only those who are approaching complete enlightenment can understand the nature of these hindrances, but descriptions are nevertheless given in the texts.

KNOWING BUDDHA NATURE

The last part of Lord Maitreya's teaching on buddha nature describes the disadvantages of not knowing buddha nature and the advantages of knowing buddha nature, each in five points.

The disadvantages of ignorance of buddha nature are dealt with first, and the first of these is self-inferiority. Without knowledge of our potential, we are likely to view our mistakes and faults as permanent and part of our essential nature, which is one of the biggest mistakes we can make. Any wisdom or realization we are fortunate to develop we may see as a form of self-delusion rather than what it truly is, an awakening of part of our ultimate potential. If we are unaware of buddha nature, we are easily convinced of our worthlessness and mistrust any good qualities we have. This is a wrong view.

The second disadvantage of not knowing about our buddha nature is ego. When we don't know about buddha nature, ego is easily developed. When we develop good qualities as a result of our positive effort, we may think we created them from nothing and in this way inflate our egos. We don't realize that we have buddha nature the same as every other sentient being, and that a good quality is a little bit of buddha nature manifesting in us, but that we are ultimately not superior to anyone else. If we don't see that others have the same potential as we do, we easily develop false pride in our small accomplishments.

Lord Maitreya describes the third and fourth disadvantages as "assert and deny." Fanaticism is an example of assert and deny. Lack of awareness of buddha nature leads to limited, narrow-minded perspectives that cause people to assert their limited views as being the only ones and deny the truth of other views. For example, if we look at Buddhist images and rituals, we might do so without ever seeing their essence, their underlying purpose. We get caught up in the outer forms. Without understanding, we deny the essence and assert the external image. If we are unable to differentiate between the external image and internal essence and make the connection between what is important and the paraphernalia around it, it can be a great disadvantage. If it does not lead to fanaticism, which can be harmful to others, it can cause the waste of a lot of time and energy due to stubbornly missing the point.

Self-attachment is the fifth disadvantage described by Lord Maitreya. When one is ignorant of buddha nature, there is a tendency to become attached to good fortune or any qualities one may develop and a reluctance to share these things with anyone. This means that whatever positive things develop in our lives will not be of benefit to others. We will become stuck in whatever we have gained, and we will eventually decline instead of improve.

Of the five advantages of knowing buddha nature, the first is joy. No matter how miserable we are, no matter how much suffering we undergo, no matter what conditions we find ourselves in, we always have joy because we know our ultimate essence is perfect. Because we know we are developing toward final realization of buddha nature, we feel absolutely secure and happy. In some of the Tantric instruction texts, this is held to be a very important attitude. A maxim translated from Tibetan into English goes, "Even if we have to suffer, we suffer happily." Suffering happily means realizing that the suffering is external and impermanent. Our buddha nature can never suffer, so suffering happily is possible. Even if we cannot avoid suffering, we have a space where we can be happy in the most difficult situations.

The second advantage of knowing buddha nature that Lord Maitreya describes is respect. We are able to respect all sentient beings, and all human beings, because they all have buddha nature. We are able to respect the environment and nature as well, because they are manifestations of buddha nature through our own interdependent sense perceptions.

Intelligence is the third advantage. When we know about buddha nature, we know about relative truth. Knowing and understanding relative truth and how to use it is intelligence.

When we know buddha nature, we know about ultimate truth. Knowing and understanding ultimate truth is wisdom. Wisdom will guide us to make the choices that speed us toward enlightenment. Wisdom is the fourth advantage.

The fifth advantage that comes of knowing buddha nature is loving-kindness and compassion. We know all sentient beings can improve because they are ultimately perfect, and their efforts to progress—as well as our own efforts to help them—will be effective eventually. All sentient beings have buddha nature. That is an incentive for us, because unless there is potential for improvement, we cannot help ourselves or anyone else, and it would be useless to try. We have compassion because we are intensely aware of the suffering all sentient beings must endure. Because of buddha nature, we can take loving, compassionate action to help. When we say the Buddhist prayer, "May all sentient beings be free from suffering and the causes of suffering," our prayer is realistic, because we know everyone has buddha nature.

Buddha nature is the most practical, helpful, and truly essential principle of Vajrayana Buddhism. We say in our Buddhist prayers that we want to liberate all sentient beings. This is a very ambitious attitude. Can we really liberate all sentient beings? Yes, we can. Can we attain enlightenment? Of course. What makes us think this is possible? Buddha nature. It is our sound basis for carrying on. We are all inherently enlightened. We just have to awaken the sleeping buddha.

—TWO—
BODHICHITTA

B ODHICHITTA IS THE ESSENCE OF ALL THE teachings of Lord Buddha, and it is especially important in Mahayana and Vajrayana practice. To call it a precious teaching is not exaggerating, because it is the source of everything we must achieve. Lord Buddha emphasized the essential importance of bodhichitta in all the Sutras and Tantras, and he spoke many times about bodhichitta as a means of transformation. Negativity can be transformed by bodhichitta, suffering can be transformed by bodhichitta, ignorance and all the five poisons can be transformed by bodhichitta. It is vital to learn and develop bodhichitta in order to achieve liberation.

Bodhichitta is a Sanskrit term. In the Tibetan language, it is translated *chang chup che sems*. *Chang* can be explained as purification, or clarification that is the result of practice. There are no boundaries and no obstacles to this clarity. *Chup* means inclusiveness. Nothing is left out. It is complete. *Che* is a grammatical conjunction. *Sems* means mind. It also indirectly represents thought, attitude, motivation, and everything involved with mind.

Another fundamental definition of *chang chup che sems*, or bodhichitta, is the desire to attain enlightenment for the benefit of all sentient beings. It may also be simply translated as the courage to obtain the highest realization. Whether it is seen as pure and unwavering dedication toward full realization and liberation for oneself and others, or understood as a thought or attitude that will be of benefit for development, a philosophical

Enlightenment mind

view, a way of thinking, a valuable principle that assists you all the way through life and lifetimes, it will lead to the same goal. It makes efforts meaningful, constantly more meaningful, until you obtain enlightenment.

There are many symbols used to describe bodhichitta. One is the lotus. In the East, a lotus is seen as the most beautiful, purest, and most perfect flower. It also grows in the muddiest, dirtiest water. Now, this beautiful lotus, although it grows in muddy water, is never stained by the dirt in which it grows. The same thing happens with bodhichitta. Bodhichitta is also developed out of a murky environment, the environment of samsara. Regardless of the negativity or evil actions in the life of an individual, once he or she develops bodhichitta, at that moment all the stains of the past are immediately purified. The Buddha himself said in the Sutras, "The validity and benefit of any expression, activity, outward appearance, or practice in the world is totally dependent on the purpose, the philosophy, and the motivation behind it." The Buddha taught about generosity, morality, diligence, and so forth, but he always emphasized the motivation behind all those so-called good and positive actions. That pure motivation is bodhichitta. The Buddha went on to say that moments before you develop bodhichitta, you might be the most evil being in the universe, but the instant you develop bodhichitta, you become the most noble, compassionate, and precious being in the universe. Bodhichitta, the purest motivation, is that powerful and important. The Buddha also said that developing bodhichitta is taking birth in the family of enlightenment.

Understanding this much, we can go on to learn about bodhichitta through practice and application. The best way to learn about bodhichitta is to consider a prayer that Mahayana Buddhists say each day:

May all beings be happy and have the causes of happiness;
May all beings be free from suffering and the causes of
suffering;
May all beings never be separated from the great joy beyond
suffering;
May they always remain in the great equanimity beyond
attachment or aversion.

This prayer is a simply stated formula for developing bodhi-chitta. It describes the four limitless thoughts. It is a combination of the four limitless thoughts and the four limitless attitudes, and the application of these four limitless thoughts and attitudes, that results in bodhichitta. As you learn this method of thought, attitude, and application, you develop bo-dhichitta. Genuinely understanding and living your life according to the four thoughts—loving-kindness, compassion, joy, and impartiality—is bodhichitta.

Jampa is the Tibetan word usually translated as loving-kindness, which is perhaps not exactly what is meant, but it is the closest English approximation. *Nying je* is translated as compassion. *Gawa* is joy. *Tang jung* is impartiality.

Between *champa* (loving-kindness) and *nying je* (compassion) there is a slight difference. *Champa* is being naturally kind and gentle, like a mother is toward her child. It is there all the time, whether or not terrible suffering is afflicting another. Loving-kindness is a pure concern, a natural caring and respect for oth-ers. We should feel toward other beings just as a good mother feels concern, caring, and respect for her child. That is loving-kindness.

Nying je, compassion, relates more to the suffering of others. An example is the attitude of a good, powerful, and kind king when he shows kindness and mercy toward his needy subjects.

Compassion is partly a deep empathy for those sentient beings that are suffering, but it is more than that. You care about them, you feel for them, you wish you could do something for them, and you actually put effort into helping them overcome their sufferings. You take responsibility for them, as a good king does. That is compassion.

Compassion and loving-kindness are the first and most important two components of bodhichitta. The prayer "May all beings be happy" expresses loving-kindness. Compassion is the wish "May all beings be free from suffering." They are very much the same, in a way. If all beings are happy, then they are free from suffering. If they are free from suffering, they are bound to be happy. It comes to the same thing, although there is a fine difference between the definitions of the two.

Joy and impartiality are the supports of loving-kindness and compassion. *Gawa*, joy, is the joy that is naturally there when you have loving-kindness and compassion, because then not only does your own happiness count, but anyone's happiness can make you happy. This joy comes from feeling good for any sentient being who is fortunate and who is doing right. You appreciate the fact that other people are enjoying a good situation, have right understanding, and are able to be effective, and you can be happy for them. You enjoy other people's happiness, instead of letting other people's happiness become your suffering, which is what can happen when negativity takes over.

When you don't have joy, when you don't have bodhichitta, then things like jealousy arise. Jealousy is what disturbs you when you hear that someone may be happier or more successful than you are. When he or she has something you don't have, you feel bad. That is actually quite a serious matter. If you have bodhichitta, developed from a strong attitude of loving-kindness and compassion, then joy arises, and you do not experience jealousy at another's good fortune. Joy is everywhere then, not only from your own good circumstances but from everywhere: "May they never be separated from the great joy beyond suffering."

We have a saying in Tibetan, "Even if you have to suffer, suffer happily." There is something in it. Think about it. A corollary would be, "Don't enjoy sadly."

Limitless impartiality, the fourth thought, means that the compassion, loving-kindness, and joy you cultivate are offered to all sentient beings equally. These positive thoughts and attitudes should not be limited to any particular object, like friends, favorite relatives, or people you admire, but should include all sentient beings. Of course, any good action begins at a personal level—at home, as the saying goes. In a healthy family, there is compassion, loving-kindness, and joy for those who are close to you within the family and those who are drawn into the family because you know and care about them. From that close group, positive feelings can move out to your neighbor, then to strangers, and eventually even to your enemies. Compassion, loving-kindness, and joy reach beyond "your kind of people," whether this means race, nationality, politics, or religion. You feel compassion for all human beings, even those who are your enemies or who perpetrate terrible crimes. You feel compassion beyond human beings to all sentient beings, such as animals or entities from realms we do not normally see. From the highest, the sentient beings of the heavenly realms, to the lowest sentient beings of hell, you learn to have loving-kindness, compassion, and joy for all of them impartially. That is limitless impartiality.

Dedication to realizing benefit for all sentient beings, limitless in number, is the core of bodhichitta. When you take the Mahayana commitment—that is, the Bodhisattva Vow—you resolve to attain enlightenment for the benefit of all sentient beings. It is a courageous commitment. In the Sutras, Lord Buddha said that sentient beings exist in space. He also said that space is endless. He taught that endless space is filled with numberless universes, and that those universes are filled with count-less sentient beings.

He described sentient beings as falling into six realms. The six realms incorporate not only physical differences, but exter-nal and internal mental conditions. The highest realm is the devic, or god realm; the lowest realm is the hell realm. Human beings are somewhere in the middle. The Buddha emphatically said that human birth is the most fortunate because human be-ings can experience both suffering and happiness, whereas in other realms it is mostly one or the other. If we take advantage of human birth, we can make a tremendous leap in our progress toward liberation. Buddha taught that it is better than any other realm for the development of wisdom and enlightenment. It is the best realm in which to learn and develop. Limitless impar-tiality is for all sentient beings, in all those six realms, through-out the universe. It is something tremendous.

In fact, all the four limitless thoughts that develop and sup-port bodhichitta are extremely ambitious thoughts. We want be-ings to be happy and also free from suffering, so it's a complete state of well-being. It sounds impossible from one point of view, but it is not just a pipe dream. It has a practical basis. Every sentient being, individually, has the potential to be free from all suffering and to be happy. More than that, every sentient being without exception has the potential of enlightenment. Lord Bud-dha said that when it comes to the ultimate potential and essence of everyone, there is no evil in existence. Of course, relatively there is evil. (Buddha himself had a cousin, Devadatta, who tried to create trouble for him all the time.) It is the potential for enlightenment of every sentient being that makes the ambitions for all sentient beings practical. It is practical for us personally as well, because each time we say the prayer for all sentient beings mindfully, we develop our own bodhichitta and get a little closer to enlightenment ourselves.

The development of these four limitless thoughts—loving-kindness, compassion, joy, and impartiality—in the management of our daily lives signifies the growth of the practice of bodhichitta. As you practice bodhichitta, your loving-kindness and compassion begin in a small way, but they should gradually become limitless. "May all sentient beings be free from suffering and the causes of suffering" is a statement of limitless compassion, which develops in stages. The first stage of compassion is the compassion you feel when you see someone in pain from hunger, illness, bereavement, or some other misfortune. That is good, but it is limited compassion. You must then look at the cause of their suffering. A person will not suffer pain unless there is a cause in his or her past of which the pain is a consequence. The cause should not be there either, but because it is, people suffer. Seeing that there is a cause is the next step.

If we look even more carefully, we can observe levels of causes of suffering. There is the immediate cause of suffering—for instance, an accident in which a person is injured. The accident is the result of something that the person did previously, perhaps in another life. The suffering of the accident is the result. If someone killed or harmed others, the result of that behavior will be some kind of suffering in this or another life. There are even subtler causes of suffering than this, however. Any kind of activities or thoughts that support attachment, anger, ignorance, jealousy, or ego all cause suffering, so it is not only some bad action that is the problem. The ego, the self, the "I"—which everyone has, even a child newborn this moment—is a primary cause of suffering. "I am hungry." "I am cold." "I am uncomfortable." "I am tired." An infant may not be able to speak, but it feels, and without language, it cries. Satisfying the child by feeding it and putting it to bed is only a temporary solution. When we wish for sentient beings to be free from suffering, then our thoughts must not be limited to the suffering itself, but must include the immediate cause and the deeper levels of cause. Treating an illness with a material medicine is not enough, because unless the causes are dealt with, the illness will not heal, or it will resurface in other ways. Limitless bodhichitta can solve the problem of suffering and the causes of suffering, because it is limitless and can reach any depth.

Viewed from the perspective of happiness, rather than suffering, bodhichitta goes beyond temporary happiness. It includes the continuum of experience from temporary, relative happiness to the ultimate fruition of positive action and realization, enlightenment. We wish sentient beings to be happy in every situation. The most basic happiness in our earthly experience is when mother, father, and child live happily together. They like each other, no hard feelings, no quarreling. Everything goes smoothly. The wish for sentient beings to be happy—bodhichitta—encompasses the most fundamental positive situation (even if it is only a good cup of tea) to the greatest, most complete enlightenment. It is not limited to human beings, nor to sentient beings of our planet, nor our galaxy of 100 million solar systems and beyond. Bodhichitta and the four thoughts that generate and support it are directed toward the happiness of sentient beings throughout the whole of space. And their happiness makes us happy. When you pray daily for others' happiness, and finally you see them happy, if you really mean the prayer, it has to make you happy. There is a big difference in the attitude. There is a big difference in the impact of the reality of life on your well-being. This is the preciousness of bodhichitta. Just understanding the four thoughts clearly and simply, you can personally recognize what you are, what you can be, and how to get there.

If we think about a part of our small world where something good is happening, we will notice this good always has something to do with somebody's dedication, compassion, loving-kindness, joy, or impartiality. The people who create good situations might not even know buddha mind exists, or may never have heard the word *bodhichitta*, but because they have the essence of it in their daily lives, they can make other people's lives meaningful. They can make their own lives meaningful. Bodhichitta is not a principle that began with the teachings of our historical Buddha; it has been there for all time.

Buddhist teachings make it clear that bodhichitta is the only cause and condition for the happiness and well-being of all sentient beings. Prince Siddhartha became Buddha because of his bodhichitta. In the Sutras, Lord Buddha Shakyamuni described his past lives. He was born in many realms: human, animal, in heaven, and in hell, and he practiced bodhichitta for many, many *yugas*, a vast length of time. He did that until he attained enlightenment, developing step by step, lifetime by lifetime, the practice of bodhichitta. Many of these stories, called Jataka tales, describe his compassionate actions.

Jataka tales are about the Buddha's incarnations in different realms, not only the human realm. One tale is about a life in which the Buddha learned a potent lesson about greed. He was born a greedy jackal, who one day came across the corpse of an elephant. He ate his way into the huge body, burrowing into the center. He decided to use it as a house as well as a meal, so there he stayed, eating and sleeping, for a long time. He stayed there until the summer dried the elephant's hide, and the hole he had entered through became too small. He could not get out. His food palace became a prison, and the jackal threw himself against the walls in vain. At long last the rains came and the hole in the carcass expanded a little, so the jackal could just barely get out. It was so tight, though, that he lost all his hair. The crisis upset him so much that he was never again so greedy.

Shakyamuni Buddha was not the only buddha to do this; all the past buddhas did likewise. All buddhas are born in many diverse situations in order to learn, become wise, and eventually practice bodhichitta. Bodhichitta, the combination of the four thoughts, is the only cause and condition for the happiness and well-being of any sentient being. It has been so in the past, will be in the future, and is the most positive action we can perform right now, at whatever level we can perform it.

The way we can do this right now is simply to ask that all sentient beings recognize what they are, who they are. May all sentient beings realize that their potential is good, not bad; healthy, not unhealthy; perfect rather than imperfect. Nothing is missing. May everyone recognize that. If they do, and act on it, a big part of our job is done. That and follow-through is the biggest step. Once it is taken, everyone who takes that step will sense the promise, almost the guarantee, of the momentum that will naturally move them forward. Until our true potential is recognized, though, even if we try to be good, it is a disheartening kind of challenge, because we doubt our innate potential and more often think that we're bad, and it is necessary to create artificial goodness. Then we try to be good, thinking the goodness is not in us, but out there. It is a false image of ourselves that is a great obstacle. Knowledge that our potential is not something we must try to create which is not there, but that it is something already within us which we work to liberate, makes all the difference.

The Buddha taught numerous techniques for liberation in the Tantras, the teachings on method. These are profound and effective, and the Buddha and all great masters always emphasized, in every Vajrayana instruction text, that the teachings should only be given to those who have bodhichitta. The profound teachings cannot be taught to those who do not have bodhichitta, because bodhichitta is the foundation. It is the heart. When you have bodhichitta, any sacred method is good and effective. When you do not have bodhichitta, the methods are useless and of no benefit. The primary practice in every Vajrayana teaching is bodhichitta. When that is there, any method you apply using that foundation works. The three parts of the Buddhist path—the view, meditation, and actions—are given life and meaning through the force of bodhichitta.

BODHISATTVA ACTION AND VIEW

Everything has a relative aspect and an ultimate aspect. These aspects are not contradictory but are two sides of one thing. It is very important to know the relative and absolute aspect of bodhichitta, otherwise you might find it difficult to practice. If we wait until we are able to practice ultimate bodhichitta, we will have to wait forever, because right now we are able to practice only relative bodhichitta. Ultimate bodhichitta is the essence and the fruition of relative bodhichitta. However, if we know and practice relative bodhichitta only, without an understanding or awareness of ultimate bodhichitta, we have a chance of becoming nice, good-hearted people who are sometimes a little emotional, but that is all—and that is not enough. This kind of limited bodhichitta cannot lead to enlightenment. One has to have the understanding of both relative bodhichitta and ultimate bodhichitta, so they can be practiced together.

The four limitless thoughts are all relative bodhichitta. The relative and ultimate aspects of bodhichitta relate to dualism. Wanting to be enlightened for the benefit of all sentient beings is dualistic thinking. We fool ourselves if we think we are nondual right now. We are nondual for short periods of time at best. Everything we do in the way of learning about Dharma, meditation, or positive actions is dualistic. We don't have to feel bad about it, because we're using our dualistic condition. We do not cheat ourselves, we are not dreaming, we are not imagining. We are handling our present condition appropriately when we deal with dualism this way.

Relative bodhichitta is the means by which we can positively relate to ourselves and others at our present level of development. That is our only possibility at this stage. Philosophically, theoretically, we can learn about many other levels, but how we understand those levels depends on our own inner development. We may learn about Buddha, talk about Buddha's qualities, about fully enlightened mind; we might even write books about it, but our depth of understanding depends on our own level of accomplishment. We cannot understand the Buddha from Buddha's level. We have to be buddhas ourselves to be able to do that. No matter what we do, learn, or think, we can only think from the level we are on. Any compassion or loving-kindness, in intention or in action, whatever we do as a bodhisattvic activity, we are doing on a relative level. That is relative bodhichitta. While we perform helpful actions for others, like giving to the poor or caring for the sick, we are expressing relative bodhichitta; but when, at the same time, we sincerely wish for all other sentient beings to be free from suffering, and use the relative as a focus for the ultimate goal, that is ultimate bodhichitta. It is a dualistic way. The duality, which begins from ego, causes ignorance, and because of ignorance we must work by means of relative bodhichitta. It starts where you are and it leads from where you are to the highest accomplishment, enlightenment.

Ultimately every sentient being is buddha. Every situation, every environment, all phenomena, even emptiness is buddha. To know that is our level of relating to ultimate bodhichitta. Knowing that, when we see people who are ignorant, who lack understanding, or who have something else going wrong with them, and we want to help, we know there is a possibility to help. The ignorance, the lack of understanding, the wrongs can be corrected. These can be corrected because ultimately people are not ignorant, nor lacking in understanding. That is how we know a negative condition can be corrected. Relatively, a person may be many terrible things, but because of buddha nature he or she can be helped. If a person were ultimately negative, there would be no way to help or improve, because there would be no potential. It would be like trying to put a cup into the earth and pour water on it and expect lots of cups to grow. It won't happen, because cups do not have this potential. On the other hand, if you have a rice seed or a flower seed and put it into the ground and water it, it will grow, because the potential is there. Sentient beings have even more potential than this, because there are no failures, no single beings who will not grow, ultimately. Every sentient being, because of innate buddha nature, has the potential to improve and eventually to manifest that buddha nature. That is the fundamental explanation of ultimate bodhichitta. Of course, there is much more to ultimate bodhichitta, which can only be understood as we practice and apply it and as bodhichitta grows.

The way we practice bodhichitta at our present stage of development is to know that we can help other sentient beings because of their great potential—ultimate bodhichitta. Even though everyone is buddha by nature, they need all the support they can get. This support is relative bodhichitta, doing everything we can to help others, or, at the very least, not to harm them. This combination of relative and ultimate bodhichitta is the best way for us to practice bodhichitta now. It is where we can start. Just wishing to do something for the benefit of others is a start. We call that "aspiration bodhichitta."

VIEW, MEDITATION, AND ACTION

The philosophy of bodhichitta, and why it can and should be generated, is the view. Once we firmly establish the correct view, then follows meditation, contemplation, and action. That is the practice. Lord Buddha said contemplation is very important. When one is developing the four limitless thoughts, the first thing one does is contemplate them. The purpose of most prayers is contemplation. The Tibetan word *sampa* and the English word *contemplation* have the same meaning, but the Tibetan word has a slight emphasis that should be explained. Contemplation has to do with understanding the meaning of a prayer when it is said, so that when you say a particular prayer, like "May all sentient beings be free from suffering," you mean it. Contemplation has to do with meaning what you pray, understanding it and meaning it. Most prayers are meant for contemplation.

There is a very fine line between contemplation and meditation, which in Tibetan is called *gonpa*. Meditation is usually a method of dealing with mind, given for the purpose of training the mind. Using those particular methods appropriately, step by step, as given in the teachings that have been passed down in the practice lineage, is meditation. Meditation is not the same as contemplating a prayer. Meditation focuses on breathing, or a specific visualization, or just watching the thoughts, or perhaps simply trying to recognize the pure quality of bodhichitta within. Meditating on such things is quite different from contemplating a philosophical tenet or aspiration through chanting, reciting, or thinking about a step-by-step prayer, such as the Bodhisattva Prayer.

The action is embodied in principles like the six *paramitas*—diligence, patience, morality, generosity, contemplation, and insight. These are applications of bodhichitta and of the four limitless thoughts, bringing them into daily activity. Performing these actions develops greater generosity, compassion, impartiality, mindfulness, awareness, and so forth. These things help you manifest beneficial activity more and more, until it becomes spontaneous. These activities, infused with bodhichitta, naturally develop wisdom. Intellectual input is information that becomes knowledge. Application of knowledge appropriately matures into wisdom, which comes from within, after deep understanding is present.

The definitions of knowledge and wisdom are appropriate to mention here. Knowledge is know-how, data, information assimilated that helps us do things. What is knowledge as far as the practice of bodhichitta is concerned? Learning the four limitless thoughts is knowledge. Applying them so that the bodhichitta essence manifests, that is wisdom. When the essence is able to manifest correctly, purely, and sharply, that is wisdom, depth of understanding. Knowledge and wisdom always progress. One can have knowledge but lack wisdom. When one develops wisdom, knowledge naturally arises.

Ten levels of bodhisattva development, called *bhumi*s, are delineated as a way of describing the constant development. There aren't actually ten levels, in one way, because the individual just grows and grows, until a development plateau is reached. Then one continues to grow. Some might envision that on arrival at one of the plateaus, they will be met by an orchestra, and a ceremony will be performed in which they will get a very nice badge and a wonderful costume and hat. With ordinary mind, it is hard to envision progress in the bodhisattva realms. The notion of ten levels is a manner of speaking about something too subtle to describe. It could as easily be a thousand levels, or a million, or five or three levels—it doesn't matter, but in the Mahayana teachings the stages are referred to as a series of ten levels.

Certain things must be done, learned, and understood to become a first-level bodhisattva. Now, to become a second-level bodhisattva, everything one has done to become a first-level bodhisattva must be undone. You become a second-level bodhisattva not by going back, but by refining the state, making it better. The knowledge that leads you to become a first-level bodhisattva becomes wisdom at that first level. But as that wisdom is used to become a second-level bodhisattva, by the time you become a second-level bodhisattva, all the wisdom of the first-level bodhisattva becomes just knowledge. That is why it can be difficult to discriminate between wisdom and knowledge. It is an example of changing, relative reality.

Real, unchangeable wisdom comes the moment an individual becomes buddha. Bodhisattva accomplishment leads to buddha-hood and uses relative knowledge and wisdom to get there. The moment you become buddha, everything is wisdom. Then there is no knowledge. Knowledge is over. Until buddhahood, every-thing is a kind of knowledge. Starting from basic knowledge, like knowing that if you are hungry you must eat, to the realiza-tion of the tenth-level bodhisattva, until buddha realization, you are involved with one or another kind of knowledge. Enlighten-ment is the final, ultimate wisdom.

Ordinary people, like most of us, understand things by means of knowledge. But in this knowledge, certain things are wisdom, because the last, most profound realization people have is their wisdom. Compared to a realized being, though, this little bit of wisdom is mere knowledge, which may be only 5 percent cor-rect, and probably less.

FIVE SUPPORTS OF BODHICHITTA

There are a few important supports for successful practice of bodhichitta, in addition to the four limitless thoughts. These are summed up in five principles. All of these five are principles to be applied to daily life. According to the Sutras, if they are prac-ticed correctly, bodhichitta will arise spontaneously, without ob-stacles. These principles govern the activity of the bodhisattva.

The first is discipline. Relatively, the individual is a mind that functions through a body and speech. All activities are initiated in the mind and are then expressed through speech or physical action. This is so with positive and negative activities alike. Negative actions like killing, stealing, lying, slander, and so forth become great obstacles to practicing bodhichitta. So one must use discipline to minimize the negative activities of body, speech, and mind.

Mindfulness is the second principle. This means being aware, mentally and physically. It is a way of overcoming ignorance. Ignorance is the cause of all obstacles, and it is fed and supported by attachment and aggression. Attachment is mental and aggression expresses physically, so it is necessary to be mindful of any thought, intention, or action that involves attachment and anger. We must learn always to be aware of the activities of our body, speech, and mind and what we are expressing through them. Mindfulness is being aware of any activity of body, speech, and mind that will create obstacles.

There are many causes and conditions that hold us in samsara, the endless cycle of rebirth and suffering. If we are not aware of them, we more easily sink into samsara. The third of the five supports of bodhichitta involves eight attitudes or patterns. Knowing about these patterns helps maintain awareness of the things that tend to lead us into more suffering. Learning about them increases our awareness and so helps us avoid pitfalls that create obstacles. Of course, we cannot overcome them all at once. We must work to overcome them gradually.

These eight are, in fact, four sets of patterns, each having two sides. The first pattern set to be aware of is the familiar feeling we have either when we get something—we are happy—or when we lose something—we are upset. The next pattern set is being happy when we are comfortable and being upset when we are uncomfortable. The third pattern set is when we hear something we like: if it sounds good to us, then we are happy, but if it does not sound good, we become upset. The last pattern set is when praise makes us happy, but insults and blame make us very upset. These eight patterns, in sets of four, are also known as the eight worldly dharmas.

These four sets of reactions are quite normal in our relative reality. They might even seem like common sense. However, if we are not mindful about these patterns, they can get out of hand and become extremely powerful negativity. Many wars have been started in this way, as we can see from a study of history. Hundreds of thousands of people have died in such wars, and if you examine the reasons for these catastrophes, it has to do with one or more of these patterns that was not mindfully monitored, was not controlled, either by an individual or by a group. Someone or some group lost something or wanted something; perhaps they did not like what they heard or were insulted and decided to take revenge or teach the other people a lesson. There was no mindfulness or wisdom, so terrible negative actions resulted. It is important always to be mindful about the potential of these patterns to develop negativity, and also to forgive. We are practicing bodhichitta, so we have to learn to forgive. We should not be too attached to good things. We also learn to be content with our situation as it is and to be forgiving.

The fourth condition that is a support for successful practice of bodhichitta has to do with discrimination between things we actually need and what we think we need, and the kind of effort we put into getting them. There are so many things that ordinary sentient beings, like ourselves, need to get by. There is a difference, though, between a real need and an imagined need. An imagined need is something we may want, but we really don't need. We put a great deal of effort into seeking and longing for lots of things we really don't need. We generate anxiety, greed, jealousy, and envy trying to get those things we think we need. We do not think very carefully about it, so we don't know if we really need it or we don't. The condition that can help us here is mindfulness that food, clothing, a place to stay, and so forth are all necessary parts of the living conditions of any life. We must always be mindful, however, that we do our best not to put unnecessary and especially negative effort into getting any of these things, and to watch carefully to make sure we are not wasting our time and creating negativity by endlessly seeking things we do not really need. This mindfulness is very important.

The last condition, the fifth, is known as right livelihood. This covers a large area because it includes everything we do. Simply stated, it means we must not earn our living by cheating others or through others' suffering. Today, ways of making a living that harm people are occupations like selling drugs, or killing beings—as butchers do, for instance. Anything that exploits either people or the environment to the detriment of all is not right livelihood. Our living conditions should not create suffering for others, and such a thing is very important for the practice of the bodhisattva, because a bodhisattva should, whenever possible, undertake activities that will be meaningful and beneficial for others. If that is not possible in every single case, then you must at least be careful not to create suffering for others through your living conditions and form of livelihood. Doing your best in your current situation is where to start. From there you can progress.

Through practicing such methods as these five particular conditions, progress naturally takes place. A sign of progress in bodhisattva practice, for instance, is development of calmness, kindness, and gentleness. A bodhisattva should develop a natural, spontaneous compassion and concern for those who are suffering, and respect and genuine loving-kindness toward others, regardless of others' conditions. Bodhisattvas develop the spontaneous habit of putting others' benefit first and their benefit afterward. If there is something good happening, you will want to share it with others first, putting yourself at the end. This kind of spontaneous habit is a sign that the practitioner is progressing on the path of the bodhisattva practice. Positive conditions of mindfulness and so forth should be continuously practiced, and they will eventually affect one's very personal well-being spontaneously.

FIVE PATHS

The progression or order of practice is clearly delineated for the practitioner of bodhichitta. It is step by step, and it is categorized into five *yanas*, or paths. In the five phases of this practice, the successful practitioner reaches different levels, or *bhumis*, of bodhisattva awareness. There are ten such levels of bodhisattva attainment that are reached, one after another, through the practice of the five paths in proper order. Bodhisattva realization is the result of correct practice of the five paths.

In all these methods, the essential principle is the application of relative and ultimate bodhichitta. Progress is achieved by realization of the five paths, through which the bodhisattva levels are achieved. The bodhisattva attains first-level realization while practicing the third path. The first path is the practice of relative bodhichitta. When relative bodhichitta becomes spontaneous in everyday actions, and ultimate bodhichitta becomes stable when meditated upon, then the first path is completed.

The second path is concerned with bringing relative bodhichitta and ultimate bodhichitta into balance. After developing spontaneous relative bodhichitta in the first path, ultimate bodhichitta becomes spontaneous in the second path. This stage is described as "the gate between samsara and freedom from samsara." The bodhisattva practitioner who reaches that level will not fall back into samsara without choice. Bodhisattva practitioners before that stage can fall back into samsara without choice. That is described as the gate.

During the third path, the practitioner has the first realization of ultimate bodhichitta. This is not intellectual understanding, but realization. It is also the attainment of the first *bhumi,* or first-level bodhisattva. The realization of the ultimate bodhichitta is the fruition of the third path.

The fourth path continues to develop the remaining progressive levels of bodhisattva realization. These levels are the process, after first realization of the ultimate bodhichitta, that leads to attainment of full enlightenment, when the bodhisattva becomes the embodiment of ultimate bodhichitta. The fourth path encompasses all the bodhisattva realizations on all the *bhumis* between the first realization of ultimate bodhichitta and full enlightenment.

The fifth path is the final practice leading up to complete enlightenment, and the last part of the fifth path is the moment before the final enlightenment. After attainment of tenth-level bodhisattva realization, a few additional stages are described, the final process through which the bodhisattva becomes a buddha. A buddha is one who attains the full realization of the ultimate bodhichitta and becomes the embodiment of it, having the limitless and spontaneous ability to benefit sentient beings infinitely.

These five paths may be practiced right now by persons like ourselves in an application of bodhichitta in our lives called the five strengths. A strength is something that will never become exhausted, that can go on and on until enlightenment. It is inner strength.

The first strength is described in the phrase "I will attain enlightenment for the benefit of all sentient beings." If the meaning of enlightenment, of "I," of sentient beings, and so forth is fully understood, that is the first strength. It is something that, once understood, will not fade.

The second strength comes after one honestly makes the commitment to attain enlightenment for the benefit of all sentient beings. It gives a drive, a momentum, that will help one go on with activities related to the first strength.

The third strength arises as that momentum continues. At that point, everything becomes like a seed. Actions in the present become the seed for the next creation, and that particular creation will become another seed. Every action and creation becomes a seed. From another point of view, it is karma. Karma means causes and conditions, so everything that is done now is a cause and condition for later events. Everything that is happening now has a condition that is related to the past.

The fourth strength can be explained by a Tibetan proverb: "When I make a journey of a million miles, I might miss my step, and slip many times, but I will put my feet back on my path." We will all make mistakes; it is expected. We do not want to, but we will. Sometimes we might make terrible mistakes, big ones. The important thing is that we should learn from our mistakes, and we should not try to lie to ourselves. We should not try to brainwash ourselves that something that is our fault is not our fault. We make mistakes, so we learn from them. The best thing to do is say, "This was a mistake." Very simple. Acknowledge it, learn from it, get back on the track, and go on. You become invincible then, because there is nothing that can destroy you. Every mistake you make, recognize it and go on. You learn from mistakes. Any bad situation becomes good in this way, because it helps you see all those mistakes that cause the negative circumstances in your life and the lives of others. The fourth strength is acknowledging our faults and learning from them.

The fifth strength is to let go of everything, every moment. This requires a little explanation. When you do something good, if you don't let go of that, you'll get stuck there. An obvious factor is the pride we might have in something we have done, which can lead to arrogance and other attitudes that become roadblocks stopping our progress forward. We get stuck there. To avoid this trap, we dedicate anything positive that we are able to do to the well-being of others. We don't think about it, we just appreciate it and then leave it for everyone.

Dedication of merit is an important part of every practice in Vajrayana Buddhism. It is always emphasized that if you do not dedicate merit, your good deed is not complete. Every prayer or practice has three parts: the beginning, the refuge, and bodhichitta. We remind ourselves, in the refuge prayer, of the Buddha, his teachings and his followers, and then we contemplate the four limitless thoughts that generate bodhichitta. The actual practice being done is the second part. The third part, at the end, is the dedication. Dedication simply means that you say, "I dedicate this merit, this wisdom, for the benefit of all sentient beings." And you can add, "So I will attain enlightenment for the benefit of all sentient beings." The fifth strength is dedication of merit.

These five strengths cause bodhichitta to increase, becoming complete and strong, so that its momentum continues nonstop.

One encouraging statement in many Mahayana sutras and commentaries (like the *Prajnaparamita-sutra,* the *Lotus Sutra,* and the *Lankavatara-sutra*) is that if you have pure bodhichitta, the four limitless thoughts, and the five strengths all together, then even if you are not doing anything, your bodhichitta naturally increases. It says, "Every pulse beating in your body, every breath you take, becomes practice." The reason is that at that point you are the bodhichitta, and therefore you are the bodhisattva.

— THREE —
REINCARNATION
AND KARMA

R EINCARNATION AND KARMA ARE INTERRE-
lated subjects that pertain to every life. Each moment is a
continuation of the previous moment, in the Buddhist view, and
this moment-to-moment continuation can seem endless. Reincarnation, simply stated, is the continuation of the mind.

There are different levels of reincarnation—the reincarnation
of ordinary human beings and of sentient beings in other realms,
such as animals, gods, spirits, and bodhisattvas. The ultimate
rebirth is the *nirmanakaya* of buddha, that is, the physical manifestation of buddha. This word, *nirmanakaya—tülku* in Tibetan—has a specific definition. Literally, it means "emanated
body." Reincarnation applies to all beings, but the term *tülku*
refers to incarnations of certain accomplished practitioners, full-
fledged bodhisattvas, and buddhas. These incarnations have
only one purpose, to serve sentient beings.

A simple definition of reincarnation is continuation of mind.
The same mind incarnates in different bodies. Mind takes birth
again and again in various physical forms. Because of this, in
Buddhism, when we talk about death, it is clear that it is not the
mind that dies, but the body. Death is relevant only to the body.
The mind does not die. These two points are important to grasp
at the beginning.

The moment of death is a powerful moment. If at the moment
of death a person—just an ordinary person—has strong devotion, compassion, and clarity, this state of mind will have great
and positive influence on his or her future rebirth. If there is

The myriad beings are formed from karma

negativity at the moment of death, such as anger, rejection, fear, whatever, it will have a tremendous negative effect on future incarnations. So the moment of death is an extremely important subject to consider in connection with reincarnation.

Generally speaking, reincarnation of ordinary sentient beings may be divided into two kinds, although it is important to remember that each individual is a unique case. There is the ordinary death without anything positive or negative during the moment of death. People who experience this kind of death will reincarnate with their past karma in complete control, because there has been no special influence during the moment of death. If there is a strong influence of a positive or negative sort, then that will override past karma. That is the second category of reincarnation, in which positive or negative thoughts direct the individual mind into a more positive or more negative rebirth.

The reincarnation of a bodhisattva is somewhat different from that of an ordinary sentient being. Bodhisattvas are beings who have been practicing bodhichitta successfully, and who have taken the Bodhisattva Vow, which means they have committed themselves to achieve enlightenment for all sentient beings as well as themselves. That is a bodhisattva by definition. There are advanced practitioners and bodhisattvas who have attained first-level bodhisattva realization. There is a difference between these two. Advanced practitioners who have not yet attained the first *bhumi* will, because of their good motivation, reincarnate in situations in which they can continue the practice of bodhichitta. They have taken the bodhisattva commitment, and, according to the strength of their bodhichitta, their reincarnations will have more or less bodhisattva activity. These individuals might be called ordinary bodhisattvas, because they have not actually attained the first *bhumi*.

According to the Sutras, once a bodhisattva has achieved first-level realization, his or her manifestation is no longer limited in the same way. The Buddha taught that a first-level bodhisattva can manifest in one hundred locations at the same time to help sentient beings. It can be in one hundred different galaxies, or in one hundred different locations of one country. From the first-level up to the tenth-level bodhisattva, the ability to determine the reincarnation for the purpose of benefiting sentient beings increases, and so constitutes another category of reincarnation, the bodhisattva incarnation.

In the Tibetan Vajrayana Buddhist tradition, we have *tülkus*. Vajrayana has methods of locating reincarnated teachers, and using these methods any incarnate teacher may be found, not only a religious master's reincarnation, but anyone's reincarnation. Of course, if the person reincarnates in another universe, it would be impossible to bring such a *tülku* back, but if the person is born in the vicinity, the reincarnation can be found. This method is never used for finding anyone but religious masters. It is not used for finding ordinary people, political leaders, or kings. It is used to find only spiritual leaders, a tradition that has not been broken up to now.

Not all the religious masters are recognized, either. Some *tülkus* return a certain number of times and are no longer found after that. Certain very great masters reincarnate without being officially recognized. There are valid reasons for this, related to the bodhisattva activity of each individual master.

Most Vajrayana Buddhist establishments have at least one reincarnated teacher, or *tülku*. This usually begins when a great and saintly teacher establishes a monastery and a particular discipline and attracts a circle of followers. When that master passes away, his or her reincarnation is usually found by a close associate, perhaps a disciple, or one of the departed lama's teachers, if any are still living. The disciples will raise the *tülku* under the guidance of the main disciple of the late master or the incarnation of the teacher of the late master. In time the reincarnated lama again becomes the head of that monastery, to continue beneficial activity. That is how the system of *tülkus* functions. The same master, and some close disciples who are also masters, reincarnate again and again to ensure the continuation of the teaching in that monastery. There were once several thousand monasteries in Tibet, about 80 percent of which had at least one *tülku*.

Reincarnation is part of the endless phenomena manifesting since beginningless time. Likewise, reincarnation of bodhisattvas and great masters has always taken place. The recognition of such incarnations who bear the same title and continue in the same seat is found only in Vajrayana Buddhism—in recent recorded history, anyway. At other times and in othes places, *tülkus* appear and are recognized for the special qualities they manifest in their lives, but no specific line of *tülkus* is established. The system of recognition of *tülkus* is unique to Vajrayana. The first incarnate lama to bear the same name, lead the same lineage, and guide the same monastery and disciples was the first Karmapa, Dusum Khyenpa, who left instructions with his disciples about how to find him in his next rebirth.

The buddha *nirmanakaya,* the manifestation of buddha, is different from the incarnation of a bodhisattva. Buddha *nirmanakaya* is beyond any kind of limitation. Even the tenth-level bodhisattva has a certain amount of limitation. A tenth-level bodhisattva has a limited number of manifestations. It is an extremely large number, but limited. A buddha has no limit. All bodhisattvas have a particular number of emanations that they are capable of manifesting, depending on their level—the first level is 100, then it goes up for each successive level. The buddha is beyond limitation and can continue to manifest infinitely for the good of all sentient beings.

Buddha *nirmanakaya* is like space. Space encompasses everyone and everything. It is not limited to one planet or galaxy but embraces all phenomena. Space is limitless. If you build a solid concrete block, space does not go anywhere. If you demolish it, space is still there. Space does not come from anywhere. It is not something we can pinpoint; it is all-pervasive. Buddha activity is like that. It is limitless. It is beyond duality. It occurs wherever there are the causes and conditions to support it. If all sentient beings in the entire universe at the same time wholeheartedly pray to the Buddha, the Buddha's blessing will come to each of them equally at the same time. A buddha will not have any difficulty with bestowing that many blessings, since the buddha is beyond any kind of limitation. When a buddha manifests to sentient beings who are above first-level bodhisattva realization, the buddha takes form in what is called the *sambhogakaya*. This may be described as the body in which beings at a lower level, primarily bodhisattvas, perceive a buddha. Beings at different levels of development have different perceptual capabilities. A simple analogy is seeing in a crowd the face of someone you know. You are acquainted with the person and recognize him or her because of your knowledge. You know the signs which indicate that person. When confronted with a buddha, if you are not acquainted with the subtleties of manifestation, you would not know you had encountered a buddha. When a buddha manifests to beings below first-level bodhisattva, it is by way of *nirmanakaya*, but limitless *nirmanakaya*.

To understand reincarnation and karma, we must look at the sentient beings, their experiences, and their surroundings from the Buddhist point of view. There is a particular term used in Buddhist texts to describe all these phenomena: illusion. The texts tell us the life of an ordinary sentient being, including the surroundings, events, and conditions, is illusion.

There are three types of illusion explained in the Tantric texts. The first and longest illusion is the one that lasts from beginningless time until the sentient being attains enlightenment. It is called the illusion of samsara. The second illusion lasts from birth until the death of each sentient being. It lasts one lifetime and is called the life illusion. The shortest illusion is the one that comes during sleep, from the time of falling asleep until waking. It is called the dream illusion. All three are equally effective illusions, the only difference being the length of time they last. That is a way of looking at the whole of existence from a simplified Tantric point of view.

Each of these three illusions has one thing in common that holds it together, like rosary beads held by a cord. The illusion of samsara is held together by the concept of "I." No matter whether birth is taken as a human or an animal, in hell or in heaven, always there is "I." Until enlightenment is reached, there is "I." The illusion of any lifetime is sustained by the particular karma that manifests for the individual. Karma is created by and centers on individual ego. The third illusion, the dream, depends on the individual's subconscious mind. The content of the subconscious mind is what manifests in the dream. What that means, simply, is that you cannot dream something that has nothing to do with you, either directly or indirectly. Sometimes dreams are precognitive, because of strong subconscious links with patterns of events, which might also be called intuition. It is possible to become obsessed by dreams if you think about this too much. You might become worried about or somehow caught up in your dreams, and that is not so beneficial. The dream comes from the individual subconscious. It is the individual ego that holds the dream illusion together.

These three illusions are contained within the self, and they are all related, in some way, to "I." Reincarnation has to do specifically with one illusion, the life illusion, and its continuation to the next life illusion. Between the life illusions there is an important period, called an intermediate period, which will be discussed in detail later.

Reincarnation answers many questions. Why is one person wealthy and another poor? Why is someone seriously ill and another healthy? Why do people look, think, and live differently? Why is one person born in a war-torn country while another person is born in a peaceful one? When each person incarnates, the lifetime is a manifestation of individual karma—that is, causes and conditions—created in past lifetimes. That is the cause of whatever situation a person is experiencing now. Understanding this is important background for understanding the entire teaching of the Buddha.

Karma and reincarnation are at the level of relative truth. Even though an individual is in a certain circumstance—maybe a bad circumstance—at the same time there is the potential to become enlightened. Everyone has equal potential to become enlightened. That is ultimate truth. That is why it is worthwhile trying to clarify and correct misunderstanding in ourselves and others. If conditions are right, and if others compassionately try to help a person, that person's wisdom can increase. An evil person can become a kind one. Everyone is ultimately perfect, a buddha. Relatively, though, everyone has plenty of imperfections until a certain level of realization is attained. Reincarnation and karma allow us to work toward realization at the relative level. They are, in a certain sense, tools for our progress.

There are misunderstandings about karma. Many people think karma is unchangeable. They say, "Oh, it's karma," and then give up. But why does that happen? This attitude is the result of thinking that karma is ultimate. Ultimately speaking, karma does not exist, but relatively speaking, everything is karma, so karma is relative truth. It is relative, so it is changeable. It is not absolute. If karma were ultimate truth, a buddha could never exist, because how could anyone become buddha? It would be impossible if karma were irrevocable, ultimate truth. It is always taught in the Sutras, in Vinaya, in Abhidharma, in

Tantra, that karma is relative truth. No matter what kind of "bad karma" we have, there is always a way out.

THE WHEEL OF LIFE

The Sutras say Lord Buddha taught about the interdependence of cause and effect. An important teaching explains this. It is called the twelve links of interdependent origination. This teaching clearly sets out the whole process of continuation of illusion in the larger picture of the cycle of rebirth, samsara; in the shorter continuation of a single lifetime; and in the continuation of every moment. A Tibetan Buddhist painting commonly seen in monastery temples visually depicts the cyclical samsaric illusion and the twelve interdependent links in a Wheel of Life.

The first interdependent link is ignorance. Because we are ignorant of nonduality due to the power of "I," we become dualistic. Being wrapped up in "I," we are blind to ultimate reality. That is ignorance, the first link in the chain of origination. In the Wheel of Life, ignorance is usually represented by a blind man.

Through ignorance, we develop the impulse to do something, to act—positive action, negative action, or actions that are neutral, neither good nor bad. As a result of this impulse, the next causes and conditions are created. The impulse to act is the second link of interdependent origination. A potter symbolizes impulse.

The third interdependent link is the impulse toward consciousness that comes from a beginning awareness of good and bad. In paintings this is represented by a monkey eating a peach. Tasting samsaric experience creates the impulse, provides the food, for consciousness to develop. This third interdependent link enables the consciousness to become solid enough to continue into the future.

The fourth link is consciousness. Consciousness, represented by two men in a boat, brings with it the manifestation of conditions, which includes outside phenomena, like the elements and other diverse and dualistic forms. Each aspect of consciousness is somehow involved with environmental mechanisms.

The fifth link is sense perception, the six senses. Because of further dualistic division, eye/form, ear/sound, tongue/taste, skin/touch, and nose/smell become more solidified. This is depicted on the Wheel of Life as six empty houses.

The sixth interdependent link is usually termed contact. It is the meeting of sense and sense-object, when the senses become strongly developed dualistically. It is the desire to touch or connect with sense-objects, and it is represented by a man and a woman making love.

This leads to the seventh link, which is the result of contact. It is the feeling of pleasure or pain. When there is touch or contact, then you feel. If it is good, you will like it; if it is bad, you won't like it. A sound, a smell, anything can cause pleasure or pain. Then there is the further development of this link: when somebody praises you, you are happy, and when somebody insults you, you are upset. This, in a way, is a separate development, but is considered part of the seventh link. In paintings it is represented by a person blinded by arrows in both eyes, because such feelings can overwhelm us and blind us to the actual nature of the situation.

The eighth link is attachment and desire, which is always wanting more. For this reason it is represented in paintings as people drinking. It results from the further development of dualistic feeling. The individual becomes attached to particular forms, particular tastes, particular touches. There is a strong desire for more. Along with this attachment and greed for things you like comes an aversion for things you dislike, and fear that you will lose what you have. So it is not just one-sided. You become attached to fear as the other side of greed. You cannot give up something you want to have, but you also cannot give up what you don't want to have. Both extremes are considered attachment.

The ninth link is pursuit of objects of desire or refusal of objects of aversion. It is shown in paintings as the aggressive grasping of a monkey grabbing fruit. This can also operate in reverse, where fear or aversion is developed toward things that are good for you, and you refuse them. Or if something is not good for you, even very harmful, attachment and greed for it may still develop, so that no matter what, you will do what you can to get it. Drug addiction is an example of this. Grasping and taking is the result of the eighth link, which develops attachment and greed and gives rise to the impulse to go after the objects of attachment.

The tenth link may be translated as becoming; it is the accumulation of more solidified karma that results in future situations, desire, attachment, and grasping. It opens the door for continuity of causes and conditions, and it paves the way for birth in one of the six realms of existence. It is symbolized by a pregnant woman.

The eleventh link is the fruition of the causes and conditions that have been created by the previous interdependent links. This is birth. Depending on the karma, causes, and conditions, the individual is born in one of the realms into which sentient beings are born. The human realm offers the best opportunity for realization. Birth could also be in the realms of gods, *asuras*, animals, hungry ghosts, and hell-beings. When conditions have ripened, birth takes place. It is depicted on the Wheel of Life as childbirth.

The twelfth link of interdependent origination is decay and death. When physical birth takes place, old age and death naturally follow. Birth is the beginning of death. Death is the beginning of the cycle all over again. A corpse represents this link on the Wheel of Life.

The first link, ignorance, the eighth link, attachment, and the ninth link, grasping, are considered to describe the three defilements. A rooster, representing grasping; a snake, representing desire and attachment; and a pig, representing ignorance, are depicted in the center of the Wheel of Life. The second link, impulse to action, and the tenth link, becoming, are categorized as action, or karma. In the Wheel of Life this link is shown as a circular rim around the central three defilements, one side of which depicts people experiencing good circumstances and the other side people experiencing bad circumstances. The third, fourth, fifth, sixth, seventh, eleventh, and twelfth links are categorized as foundations for the suffering of samsara. It is another way to view the twelve links of interdependent origination, in a different order. The entire Wheel of Life is held in the grasp of a demon, Yama, the Lord of Death, signifying that no matter what realm or what circumstances, the cycle of rebirth continues. Outside the entrapment of the wheel, the Buddha shows the path toward freedom from rebirth and suffering.

This is reincarnation as it is taught in the Buddhist Sutras and Tantras. Reincarnation is clarified in the Tantric texts, along with the process of transition from this life to the next life. It is helpful—and important—to have some idea of the Tantric perspective on the human mind and body. From the Tantric point of view, the body and mind have many levels. There is more to it than the body and mind we perceive with limited understanding in ourselves and others around us. The bodies and minds we perceive form a small part of the picture.

There is a macrocosmic body, which includes all that we see and experience within it. The whole universe is our body, because we are in it. It is our greater body, and whatever happens in any part of this universe affects us, although we may not be fully conscious of how. That is how Tantric astrology can be useful in people's lives, because it is a method of finding out about these universal events and dealing with them. If somebody puts the hand of your immediate physical body in a fire, it hurts. The same thing is also true with the greater body. Whatever happens in any part of our universe affects us. We might experience it as a bad mood, as reverses or good fortune in our finances or personal relationships, or as spiritual lapses or progress. Astrology can determine things that go on in our immediate galaxy and solar system, but the influences beyond that also affect us. In Tantric texts, this macrocosmos is called "third thousand" and means 100 million solar systems.

The "second thousand" is smaller than the third thousand. It represents 1,000 times 1,000, or 1 million. Whatever happens in this part of the universe affects us more than events in the greater macrocosmos. Events in the "first thousand," the 1,000 immediate solar systems that surround us in every direction, affect us very strongly. What happens in our own solar system affects us most immediately. Of course, whatever happens on our planet has a profound effect on us. Now that we are able to analyze environmental degradation and its effects on life forms, we are experiencing just how true this is. There is earthly scientific proof of these effects of our environment on us, and our effects on the environment.

After considering the descending spheres of manifestation, the Tantric texts then examine how events within the individual body affect the mind. At the level of the immediate physical body we inhabit as human beings, there is an outer body, an inner body, and a subtle body. There are many levels of the body. Those born in the human realm of this earth have a particular type of outer body, inner body, and subtle body. The outer body can be positive or negative. The inner body is more positive than negative. The subtle body is positive. The mind, buddha nature, is perfect.

Breath corresponds to these aspects of the body too. Breathing is something we do all the time. In breathing there is the outer breath, the inner breath, and the subtle breath. Through meditation, recitation, exercise, and various practices the outer body may be purified as the outer breath is being purified, and the inner and subtle breaths may influence the outer body and outer breath.

The physical relationship between our bodies and our minds is developed right before we are conceived in our mothers. The connection between this particular body and mind is developed just at the moment before conception. This coming together and mingling of the nonmaterial mind and the material body is one of the most important steps in the reincarnation process.

The mind is, of itself, very subtle, but the thoughts and feelings produced in the mind are not as subtle as the pure nature of the mind. Thoughts and emotions are limited; mind is limitless. Thoughts are a manifestation of ignorance, which causes them to be limited. The subtlest energy of the universe is the subtlest component of physical existence. This subtle energy and the thoughts and emotions of the mind are able to connect and hold together. This subtle universal energy, along with the thoughts and emotions, combine with the power of karma, called karmic wind or air, and enter what is called the first physical substance. This first physical substance is known as the liquid body.

Under normal circumstances, the liquid body solidifies after twenty-nine days. It slowly solidifies, but after twenty-nine days the karmic air, the energy of the universe, and the emotional aspect of the mind all concentrate in the center of the slightly solidified liquid body. The karmic wind involves our fathers, our mothers, and ourselves. All the karmic connections come together. It is like the center of a cyclone. Wherever we are at that moment, even 20 million galaxies distant, our consciousness will be brought to wherever our karmic father/mother is to join with the liquid body. Our body manifests from the solidified liquid body according to the causes and conditions, the karma. This begins in what is called the central channel. It is located in the middle of the trunk of the body.

All the senses are concentrated in the middle of the body. Limbs are important, but limbs are not necessary for continuance of life. If someone cuts off our leg or hand, if we are properly cared for, we will not die. If the body is cut in two in the middle, however, or the head chopped off, we die. The center of the body is the most important part. All the channels develop from it. The outer channels include the arteries, veins, and nerves. The subtle body has its own inner channels, which we cannot usually see. All these are developed through the movement of karmic air, universal energy, and the emotional component.

There is a simple metaphor. There is a nice meadow with lots of edible roots under the ground. A family of rabbits lives on the other side of the meadow. Every day the rabbits go from their home under a bush to the meadow to eat the roots. After a while, the rabbits' footprints create paths to all the important places for food and water. As the energy moves in the liquid body, it develops all the channels and limbs, everything according to its movement. Movement traces the form.

Experts and intuitive people can read faces, palms of the hands, and the like to see the future because these physical features are the end result of the whole karmic process of connection between mind and body for a particular life.

This is a very simple explanation of how formless mind enters into the form, feeling, senses, and so forth of a physical body. The past life of a being might have been a spirit or an animal, but it may be born in this life as a human being. What is born also dies. When the mind leaves the body, that is death. Death is the death of the body, not of the mind. Mind does not die, it always continues.

THE BARDO

The life of a sentient being is made up of stages, ended by death, after which follows another stage, which in Tibetan we call *bardo*. An understanding of bardo is necessary to grasp the important processes of life and death of sentient beings. By striving for this understanding, we learn how to utilize these stages as a means toward greater realization.

The word *bardo* means "in between." When you hear about the bardo, if you know a little about Tibetan Buddhism, your first thought may be of a process that follows death, because of what you may have heard or may have read in books like *The Tibetan Book of the Dead*. While the after-death process is part of it, the bardo teachings actually describe stages that are not confined only to the time after death. Lord Buddha Shakyamuni gave the teachings on the bardo, and since that time numerous realized and learned masters have continued the lineage.

Simply, bardo describes the in-between state of things. For example, the gap in between samsara and nirvana, pure and impure, birth and death, death and rebirth is bardo. There are six aspects of bardo that include and summarize all the aspects of the samsaric and spiritual process. These six are the birth bardo, the dream bardo, the meditation bardo, the bardo of the moment of death, the bardo of the ultimate nature, and the universal or possibility bardo, which is the bardo that extends from the time of death until the time of rebirth into another life.

Birth Bardo

When a being is reborn in this universe as a sentient being, it is a coordination of the body, speech, and mind of that particular being, together, here in the world. As a result of the karma accumulated by the ego, the consciousness of a being enters into a particular realm of existence. That is the moment of the first connection between the body substance and the consciousness of that being. After that moment, the physical body and formless mind coordinate and communicate. It can be explained in terms of a human birth, although the process is the same for all beings. Because we are human beings, we can learn the most from an explanation of this coordination of existence from a human standpoint. The physical body develops according to the capability of the formless mind: according to its desire, its ignorance, its anger, its stinginess, and its pride and jealousy. The kind of consciousness a being has developed determines how the physical body will develop—whether it will be healthy or unhealthy, fully developed or underdeveloped. Some beings are complete, some are deformed, and this is the means by which it comes about. It is a complicated process.

During the first twenty-nine days of existence of physical substance inside the mother, consciousness is everywhere, permeating substance. When consciousness enters, it does not have any substance, but it relates with the most subtle substance, the air element. This energy or air substance can receive and be permeated by consciousness. When the substance becomes more solid, consciousness cannot freely move everywhere. Being unable to freely permeate this harder substance, consciousness moves into the middle of the developing substance. This becomes the central channel, or *tsa uma*. From this central channel, consciousness radiates, manifesting in all directions by means of the energy centers and subsidiary channels, *khorla* and *tsa* in Tibetan. Through these channels the influences travel, and the substance of a being develops according to its karma, from the twenty-ninth day until the birth of the child. This is how growth takes place. The birth of the child marks the complete development of all the important seats of consciousness. After birth the child continues to develop, but it develops what is already there. Nothing new is added.

At this point there is coordination of mind, senses, and the universe, of the "I" and form. Nose and smell, tongue and taste, body and touch are coordinated on the outer levels. On the inner levels, there is coordination of mind, buddha nature, and the ego, desire, anger, ignorance, jealousy, and so forth. This constellation of realized mind and hindrances or defilements is unique to the individual and is the basic relative reality that the individual will come to terms with in the life to come. It influences the future of the life. It is from this karmic pattern that the individual can learn ultimate truth.

Although in the Vajrayana teachings each atom of a human body can be seen as an expression of these patterns, the important points of focus are body, speech, and mind. Body is the solid appearance, speech is the expression, mind is the essence. The ultimate level of body, or material manifestation, is *nirmanakaya*. The ultimate level of speech, or expression, is *sambhogakaya*. The ultimate manifestation of mind is *dharmakaya*. This is the truth of the first aspect of bardo, the bardo of birth.

Dream Bardo

The second kind of bardo is the dream bardo. The principal focus of this bardo is to allow us to understand the universe, our lives, our entire experience as a dream. There are three parts to this bardo: the samsaric dream, the life dream, and the sleeping dream. The samsaric dream lasts from beginningless time until the realization of the ultimate, which is buddhahood. No matter which realm we belong to, no matter what kind of individuals we may be, we are dreaming. All dreams are ego trips, even in the animal, because they come from "I." If we are human or god, the "I" is there. We can be rich, we can be poor, we can be people of different cultures, and always we have the "I." We wake up from this "I" when we achieve enlightenment, buddhahood. That is the only time we will become completely free from "I." Buddhahood is the end of the samsaric dream.

The second dream is the life dream. The life dream is also known as the dream of karma. According to our individual actions, we experience the dream of karma. The same thing that can make us happy can also make us sad; we may sometimes hate it, sometimes love it. Sometimes it helps us, and sometimes it troubles us. Nothing is certain. Nothing is "real" or fixed as true existence. Everything changes. The same thing can affect various people in various ways. This is the life dream. It starts when we are born, it ends when we die. Another dream will start after that. The dreaming goes on as long as we take birth.

The sleeping dream is the dream of the subconscious mind, and the kind of activity in our subconscious mind will determine the content of our dreams. Sometimes we may dream about the future. Sometimes we dream about the past. We will not dream anything that has nothing to do with us, because whatever we dream is about ourselves. This is the sleeping dream. We wake up from this when we wake up in the morning. In the bardo teaching, the practice is to realize the unreality and illusion of the dream while dreaming. You gain awareness so that your dream cannot fool you anymore. You can control your dream instead of letting the dream control you. When you have this freedom completely in your sleeping dream, you will achieve a certain amount of freedom in the life dream. The miracles of great realized beings are related to mastery of the sleeping dream.

It is worthwhile to consider miracles for a moment, because they are related to the ability to control the dream. People often confuse miracles and magic. A miracle is the result of accomplishing ultimate freedom. Magic is a relative, worldly art, a kind of performance. The magician does things by learning material tricks or using a powerful energy substance, special words, or imagination and visualization. These tools are ultimately unreliable because they involve hope and fear. The desire to do a thing causes the hope to do it successfully and the fear that it may be a failure. All this is tied in to the ego, the "I." Magic is interesting to watch, but it does not benefit anyone ultimately. The magicians themselves may be full of suffering, desire, anger, ignorance, everything, but their greatness is that they know a technique. We can learn one thing from magic. It proves to us that samsara is illusion. It is because of this illusion that magic can be performed. Without illusion, nothing like magic could happen. It is a trick, the art of illusion.

The real miracle is freedom. It has nothing to do with ego. The less powerful the ego is, the more profound the miracle. People experience miracles, but they don't recognize them. The simple miracle of the profound teaching of Buddha can change a being who is suffering or who is evil into the kindest of beings in just one moment of right understanding. This miracle of simple Dharma can change the world from a disturbed place into a peaceful one. The first step is correct understanding and action: basic loving-kindness and compassion toward each other as brothers and sisters. If such a practice were universally adopted, violence and wars could not happen. Adhering to such elementary ways of relating can create a miracle that could bring the whole world peace. If beings are capable of learning and accepting this, rather than thinking about a miracle happening from out of nowhere without any effort on their part, they achieve freedom. They gain freedom in the life dream in the same way they can have freedom in the sleeping dream.

In the sleeping dream you see a fire. You recognize you are dreaming; you know you are asleep in your room where there is no fire. You see your hands in your dream, but your hands are dream hands, not physical hands. If you put your dream hands into your dream fire for five hours, it will not burn your fingers.

It is not magic, it is a kind of miracle that comes when you learn to master your situation in the sleeping dream. When this process is undertaken in the life dream, it is also a miracle and works in a similar way. The miracles of the great masters of the past were performed in this way. These masters had freedom because they realized the ultimate nature of all things. For those with such freedom, nothing makes any difference to them; they have no hopes or fears, they are detached, and that is how they are able to perform miracles. Miracles are not limited, they are limitless, and when one has the freedom of the sleeping dream and then the life dream, it is the beginning of mastery of the samsaric dream. The total development of freedom and the awakening from the samsaric dream is known as buddhahood.

Meditation Bardo

The third kind of bardo is the bardo of meditation, which may be divided into three categories: the body meditation, the speech meditation, and the mind meditation. The meditative state in Tibetan is called *samten,* meaning "stable mind," and each of these aspects is a type of *samten.*

The proper way of sitting is body *samten.* Stability of the body naturally develops the meditative state. An example of the importance of the appropriate physical arrangements and their effect on the state of the mind is a temple. When we go to the temple we find that the surroundings are peaceful, the inside of the temple is clean, the Buddha image is beautiful. The simplicity brings a natural calmness to anyone who enters. In the same way, preparing and holding the body properly brings a natural calm and contributes to the meditative state. The body is the temple of the mind. The opposite extreme is a disco filled with loud music and lights, with everyone jumping around. It agitates a person and distracts from inner calm, in comparison to the atmosphere of a temple.

The right way of sitting, cross-legged, with a straight back, is not just a product of Eastern culture—although in the West, when Buddhist Dharma began to spread, people tended to look at it that way because it was not their habit and it was difficult for them. The reason for the effectiveness of this posture is that it is based on the human coordination of body, speech, and mind. Correct posture supports the central channel, which is the center of our vital force. For the mind to be at peace in the meditative state, everything must be in order; then peace becomes simple to achieve. When you eat, most people will agree that it is best to sit up straight. If you lie on a bed to eat, it can be detrimental to your health because it is possible to choke on the food that way, and it is also bad for digestion. It is natural to sit up. When you sleep, you must lie down. If you go to sleep standing up, you will fall down and may hurt yourself. Sleeping sitting in a chair is not very restful. Similarly, the correct posture for meditation is a natural posture conducive to meditation. Utilizing this posture for development of the meditative state is the body meditation.

Speech meditation is saying the proper words. All the prayers, the chanting, and the mantras have many levels of meaning. Some are just ordinary words, some are symbolic words, and all of them might be called words of speech meditation. We already examined what contemplation of the prayer generating bodhichitta can do. With the body seated in its most profound posture and the speech expressing the most profound words, an important positive link can be forged. If we say to someone, "I respect you," the person feels good. If we say to someone, "I hate you," the person feels bad, of course. This is an example of the power that words can have. A person sings a nice song with a good voice. It makes you feel good and may even calm you. If a person sings badly or expresses negativity in the song, it grates and can put you out of sorts. Compare the sound of a clear temple bell tapped in a silent shrine room and fingernails scraping on a blackboard. This is the effect of sound. Saying the right word in the right way is speech meditation.

Mind meditation involves thinking correctly. The mind rests in peace. It rests in the natural state, thinking compassion and loving-kindness toward others. Thinking in this way leads to perceiving the ultimate truth. Having devotion and confidence in those who have achieved buddhahood, and confidence in the teachings of the Buddha, bodhisattvas, and realized masters is having the right attitude, the right path, and the right guidance.

To be able to do body, speech, and mind meditation properly, you must do it not only when you sit down and meditate, but when you are walking, when you work, when you eat, when you cook, when you talk with others, when you sleep—all the time. There is always a better way to do things, to improve. We improve by having mindfulness and awareness. So the meditation bardo is the state of stable meditation involving body, speech, and mind. Extending this state beyond the time of the formal meditation period, holding the stable meditative state even when going about one's daily affairs, is a practice that can help prepare for moments of challenge, the greatest being the transitional phase between lifetimes, the moment of death.

Bardo of the Moment of Death

Before we find ourselves in the bardo of the moment of death, we should prepare for it. If we wait until the moment of death itself to get our minds ready, it will be too late. We can prepare for it beforehand by, whenever possible, doing what is helpful and meaningful and avoiding activity that is meaningless or harmful. In this way merit is accumulated outwardly and wisdom is accumulated inwardly. Whenever we are able to develop and improve, we must take advantage of the opportunity to do so. The moment of death is a moment we will all definitely have to face one day, and it is the most significant event of our lives. It is unlikely that any of the people who are reading this will still be around in 100 years. We will all be gone. Very few babies who are in their mothers waiting to be born will be here after one century. We will die, and we have to face that fact honestly. Most of us do not know when we will die, either.

The moment of our death is very important, because it is the moment of transit from this life to the next phase that leads to the next life. The judgment on us then is based on our karma, the causes and conditions we have created by our thoughts and actions in the past, and on no one else's. If we have a clear understanding and a good opportunity, we can accumulate merit and purify previous negative karma at that moment. We can do this at the moment of death better than at any other time. Right now we can pray, meditate, generate bodhichitta, and perform good acts with a certain amount of sincerity, purity, confidence, and strength, but at the moment of death the potential for this is multiplied tremendously if we have learned how to think clearly, dedicate merit, and take advantage of this special opportunity. At the moment of death, one brief thought will be more potent than years of thought in an entire lifetime. That is why it is so important to realize clearly that you are in the last moments of life, but that you are alive and facing the most serious event of that life for the purpose of your further development. Since that moment is so critical, it is helpful to know the factors that will disturb the mind.

The three things that will disturb us at the time of death are our fame, our wealth, and our relations. Attachment to our fame, our wealth, or to people we are being separated from is the biggest obstacle to clarity. When the moment of death comes, we must be ready to release everything. We must realize that we no longer need these things and that even if we were able to hold on to our money, we can take nothing with us; our money will be lying in our cold hands, useless. Fame is the same. After a short obituary on the back page of a newspaper, we will be forgotten. The people we are close to will resume their lives and carry on without us. The most important preparation for the moment of death is to have, in life, done everything to the best of our abilities, so that we have nothing to regret, no actions that make us feel sorry, guilty, or ashamed. We must have simple feelings at the moment of death. And to have these simple feelings, we must prepare beforehand, by doing whatever meaningful things we can do in our daily lives. We may utilize material belongings, reputation, or position, or we may personally perform beneficial actions for others. After performing beneficial actions, we dedicate the merit earned for the benefit of all sentient beings, wishing sincerely that all beings may be free from the sufferings of samsara, the Wheel of Life. And we also pray that, according to our capability, we may be reborn into the human realm, cultivate more virtues, and be able to achieve realization of the ultimate truth. We may also pray to be reborn in Dewachen, the Sukhavati Pure Land, where we may be instructed in the path to enlightenment by a buddha who is the embodiment of wisdom.

A person offers whatever he or she is capable of offering. If you are capable of saying, "May I go to hell and help all the beings of hell, and until they are free from hell may I remain in hell," and mean it, that is the best thing to do. The main point, though, is do what you can. Do your best.

At the moment of death, there is one special practice that can be done, and that is known as transference of consciousness, or *phowa* in Tibetan. To be able to do it requires special training over a period of time. Accomplishing this practice successfully will liberate the consciousness of the individual from lower rebirths.

Bardo of the Ultimate Nature

The bardo of the ultimate nature is the highest essence of the Vajrayana. Everything in the entire universe is a manifestation of the ultimate nature. Everything speaks ultimate nature to you, everything gives you the message, everything is introducing itself to you as impermanent. Friends come together, talk, and enjoy each other's company, but the end of their meeting is always separation. A king builds a palace, but as soon as he has finished the palace and feels satisfied at its completion, it begins to deteriorate. All that remains is for the palace to crumble and fall down, which it will certainly do in time. A baby is born and we are excited about having a new family member, but the future of that newborn is to die, since what is born must also die. In the morning we see the sun coming up. It is the beginning of the day. But it will soon go behind the mountain, and darkness will fall again. These things are what should come and what will come. That is the true nature of everything. The phenomena of existence tell you that everything is emptiness, everything is impermanent, everything is only a temporary manifestation—but essentially it is the ultimate, buddha nature. To realize this is to be able to utilize the full value of the opportunity presented by each moment of our lives, and that is the bardo of ultimate nature.

Possibility Bardo

The sixth and last type of bardo is the one that is familiar to most people who have heard about bardo. It is the state in between the death of this body, in this life, and rebirth in the next life. When any beings of any realm pass away from their current life into the intermediate state, the length of time spent in the intermediate state and the type of experience the being has are totally dependent on that being's karma.

The bardo after death, between death and conception in a

new body, is an important part of the process of reincarnation. Many teachings are given about this, such as the tantra entitled *Liberation by Hearing*. This and many other tantras explain about the after-death process. This period is particularly significant in the death of the human being, and it is a teaching for human beings.

The bardo after death begins at the moment of death and ends at the moment of conception in the next incarnation. The maximum period of the bardo is forty-nine days. The minimum can be a split second, but the longest is forty-nine days. It is clearly stated in the texts that this applies to the human beings of our planet earth.

Death, in its process, is the reverse of conception. We go out of the body in the same way we entered it. Everything that happens when we come in has to happen when we go out. The only way to get out of your house is to go through the door, the same door you came in by. If it is a normal, comfortable death, not an accident or something of that sort, the first sign that death is imminent is when the earth of the individual body dissolves into the universal earth. At this point the person feels extremely heavy and cannot move. Then the air of the body dissolves into the universal air, so it becomes hard to breathe. All these are signs by which we may know that life is leaving the body. The physical earth dissolves into the universal earth, air dissolves into the universal air, water dissolves into the universal water, and fire dissolves into the universal fire, with signs for each phase. The event of death is the absorption of our physical elements into the elements of nature.

All the sensations, feelings, and eventually the physical form that developed after mind connected to the body at conception return to where they came from. The limbs become cold and lose feeling first. The center of the body still stays warm, so focus flows to the middle. Inside the central channel, the positive energy of the universe and the negative energy of the universe, which are white and red, collide. Then you might say the mind faints, the body and mind become unconscious. It is the moment of final absorption.

Death and the stages after death are profound upheavals in our experience. It is one reason why we do not remember what happened in our past lives. It is like a great explosion that causes amnesia.

If you have pure devotion and pure compassion, if you are a very good meditator, and if you can be aware of that state at the critical time, then you have a real opportunity at the moment of death to attain enlightenment, because at that moment you are completely free from all the karmic connections of this lifetime. That moment of collision and fainting can become enlightenment, because nothing is there but your buddha nature, if you can recognize it. If a person does not have compassion or devotion, normally he or she will be afraid, or perhaps angry or resentful, and then, of course, this chance will be missed. The best death is the natural death, because it is easier for the mind to be without fear, greed, anger, or resentment, which is the way to die properly. Meditation and beneficial practices can help us cultivate the necessary strength of mind. We do not have to waste our natural death. For those who are great meditators, who are aware and unafraid, with trained minds, it is the chance of a lifetime, a chance for enlightenment. This initial period can be long or short. It can be as long as three days or as short as a moment. It depends on the individual. This particular stage of the bardo is called the first clear light.

The second clear light comes when you awaken from that unconsciousness. It is at this point that an individual has an opportunity to take birth in the Pure Land. The Pure Land practice in the Vajrayana teachings has outer, inner, and secret levels. It is a buddha realm, and not easy to imagine with our ordinary minds, but it is a place where individuals may take birth. For the sake of simplicity, we may look at it as a physical outer rebirth in the Pure Land. When you wake up from the unconsciousness after the event of death, because of devotion and compassion it is possible to become a first-level bodhisattva by taking birth in the Pure Land of Amitabha, who is the Dhyani Buddha of the Lotus family. There are many pure realms into which an individual might be born a bodhisattva; the Amitabha Pure Land is one of them. And there are outer, inner, and secret levels as well. It is possible to be born into the outer level of Amitabha Pure Land as a first-level bodhisattva as soon as you awaken from the faint of death, if all the conditions are right, and there is sufficient accumulation of merit.

If an individual does not attain enlightenment at the first clear light, or is not born as a bodhisattva into Amitabha's Pure Land, the consciousness goes out of the physical body. It has to go out of the physical body because the karmic relationship with this physical body and the mind has finished. As consciousness goes out, the individual enters the second bardo stage. The first stage of bardo comprises the first clear light and second clear light. After that the second-stage bardo begins, the stage in between leaving one body and the next rebirth.

Right now, while we are alive in a body, our senses and consciousness work through the physical vehicle designed by ourselves, by our karmic causes and conditions. We can hear from the ears on only two sides; we can smell only from our noses; we can only see forward and to the side in a limited way, and if we want to see behind us, we have to turn around. During this second stage of bardo, everything is vivid; input comes from everywhere. Without the limitation of physical ears, you can hear everything. All the senses are freed from the limitations of a material body. Right now, what we hear, see, touch, and taste depends on our sense organs. The input and experience are focused there. At the time of the second bardo there are no such limitations, so there is total sound and light. Everything becomes sound and light, like a great explosion that never stops.

According to sutras such as the *Great Liberation Sutra* and tantras such as *Liberation by Hearing,* in that stage, if you recognize you are dead, that you are in the bardo state, that all these sounds and lights and apparitions are just a part of you, and it is your karma, your consciousness, manifesting, and if you are able to observe the buddha nature, or even if you are able to concentrate on any buddha or bodhisattva, you can be liberated at that time very easily. The Buddha said recognizing even that much is enough for liberation.

Generally speaking, for ordinary persons who have no merit or do not have good practice, it would be very difficult to think of anything, and at worst it can be the most frightening experience imaginable. It might be compared to falling from an airplane at 50,000 feet. You have a piece of paper and brush, and before you hit the ground, you have to execute your best calligraphy. It will be that difficult. Those who have pure devotion and pure compassion, when they are in such a situation, may not remember much of what to do, but if they remember Amitabha or another buddha or bodhisattva, it can help tremendously. This is why it is so important to do practice during one's lifetime, to prepare for this difficult transition. For people who practice diligently when they are alive, when death comes and this stage of the bardo is reached, if fear arises it invokes devotion and compassion. That is the great chance.

After this stage, the individual emerges from all the sound and light and develops an identity called the bardo body. In the period of time closest to the past life, the bardo is full of feelings, thoughts, and perceptions of the past life. This middle period is an unclear and obstructed time. The last half of the period is filled with impressions of the next life as the sensations of the previous life recede. In between these two, in the middle, there is a gap that is a little bit like the past and a little bit like the future. If somebody is a man in this life, and is going to be a woman in the next life, then in between that will be a physical, mental, and emotional threshold of the different physical manifestations. If you take an extreme example such as a human and an animal, there will also be that middle threshold period. It is another small bardo, in between, where there is a little confusion, but it also offers another chance for great liberation.

During this time of transformation from the past life into the future life, if prayers and meritorious actions are performed by surviving friends and family with strong devotion and faith, the being in the bardo may be influenced beneficially, according to the being's karmic capacity. When an individual is in the bardo, it is similar to when he or she hears teachings in life. If there is the capacity to understand, the teachings will be understood and a degree of realization is possible. At the time when a being is in the bardo, these prayers can have good effect, because the bardo is a clear state without the obstacles of body and speech. It is only mind itself that holds the consciousness with its karma and its poisons. Mind by itself is much easier to influence. So the people left behind have a responsibility and an opportunity to benefit the departed by their prayers. It can be a very important act of kindness.

The third-stage bardo is the last phase of the bardo after death and before incarnation. At that time the intense sound and light experience recurs, just before reentry into an incarnation, at the point of stepping from the stage of bardo into the stage of life, where the whole process of living and dying repeats itself. The texts describe all the manifestations that are experienced at this threshold, such as peaceful and wrathful deities, the lights that represent the various realms of birth, and so forth. If the individual has great development, there is also a chance for liberation here. If there is strong compassion and devotion, and the mind is not overwhelmed by exposure to all the bardo phenomena, it is possible to choose the next incarnation at that moment—if there is strong compassion, devotion, recognition, and realization. Otherwise the karmic wind just blows you wherever you belong karmically. That is the last chance as far as the bardo period is concerned. Then the bardo is over.

The possibility bardo is the connection between one life and the next life. The bardo process is a process of reincarnation. When you are reborn in the next life, that is the process of reincarnation being materially manifested. So this period is extremely important, so much so that the Buddhist teachings always encourage the individual to prepare for that moment. If enlightenment cannot be attained in this lifetime, then at least prepare for that moment when there is the best chance to attain it. Even if one is not liberated at the moment of the first clear light, there is still a greater chance of being born in an appropriate, positive incarnation in the future life if there is meritorious karmic accumulation and practice from this lifetime. Death is a normal result of taking birth, so we should be able to handle it properly when it comes.

A few things may be said for practitioners who would like to do something to prepare for the bardo. One important point always to remember is impermanence. We never know when we will die. Doctors might give us an estimate, but we cannot know for sure, so even then death can be unexpected. Acknowledging impermanence will help tremendously in getting ready for the moment of death. When it happens there will be less shock, fear, and resentment. If we are deeply aware of impermanence, these negative states of mind will not occur, because we know that when death happens it happens, even if we do not like it; it doesn't help to complain. It is better to be able to accept it so that you can handle it smoothly and correctly, rather than being upset, and allowing that upset to influence you at this critical moment. Always remember impermanence.

Some people think that remembering impermanence will make them disorganized or will be bad for business. That is not really true. People can be better businessmen or businesswomen if they remember impermanence in the right way. It is always good to have several contingency plans.

Another point: Do not overlook any opportunity to perform positive deeds or avoid negative deeds. It is good to take such opportunities seriously, because it can be very important at the end. If we see something good that can be done, but if we forget about it, or just don't take advantage of it, we lose that opportunity unnecessarily. If we see negativity that we can avoid, but are lazy and don't bother about it, and then go ahead and get involved in it, that is also an unnecessary waste. It is much better to take positive and negative things seriously. Avoid as much negativity as possible and perform as many positive acts as you can. If somebody in the street wants you to give some money, and you have fifty cents, give it, because fifty cents is not really much. If you give it and the person can use it, that creates good karma. We should not deny even small things. If a fly jumps into your glass, don't just take it and pour it into the sink, drowning the fly. Take the fly and throw it out the window before pouring the water into the sink. It's simple. It doesn't really take much effort, and doing it won't make you a fanatic. Someone might think, "What's the use in saving this fly? I eat meat." Of course you may eat meat, but you might as well save this fly as well. It is better to eat meat and save a fly than do nothing positive at all. Some people offer prayers for the sentient beings they eat, which is a good practice.

Dream practice is also considered very helpful in preparing for the bardo stage, because the bardo is a little bit like a dream. The brief dream illusion, of course, is not comparable to the enormity of the bardo, but there is a relationship that can be useful for practice. When we sleep and dream, we should try to achieve and maintain mindfulness and awareness enough to recognize that we are dreaming. This will not disturb our rest. It might even help us rest better while dreaming, because if a tiger chases us in our dreams, we will know it is not serious, and we will not be exhausted when we wake up. Instead, we might watch what that tiger does. It might spring or bite, but nothing will happen to us. The tiger might talk to us, or we might become the tiger, or the tiger might fall asleep. Cultivating awareness while dreaming is useful in preparing for the possibility bardo.

Practices like *phowa,* the transference of consciousness, or even the *phowa* blessing, will be helpful, as well as receiving empowerments related to the bardo. Any Dharma practice is very beneficial. Any good thought, good inspiration, or helpful actions toward others will be very beneficial. If you can meditate on the nature of the mind, so as to deeply contemplate and experience the nature of mind, that will be of tremendous benefit. That is one of the most important parts of meditation, actually, recognition of your own buddha nature. Even if it is only a glimpse of recognition, it will really be worth it.

All this is great preparation for the bardo. If you read *The Tibetan Book of the Dead* carefully and contemplate it—not obsessively, just calmly and sensibly read through and contemplate it—it might also be of assistance, because it gives you an idea of what to expect and what is supposed to happen. What you learn about it now will be useful later.

One last point. We can advantageously relate right now through our physical senses to the universe we will experience so vividly in the bardo, using a subtle exercise. It is called hearing the sound of nature. It is done at a peaceful time, when surroundings are quiet. There is an enormous sound that goes on all the time, but because we are always thinking, talking, or otherwise occupied, we never hear that sound. When we are quiet, we can hear a little bit of it. Concentrate on that sound. Calmly try to maintain that sound, at least when resting at home. It will help tremendously, because that is one of the sounds we encounter during the bardo.

Understanding reincarnation, the reasons for it and its processes, is critical background for understanding Buddhist Dharma. Normally everybody views death as a very negative thing, often with fear and aversion. It isn't negative. It is a significant part of the process leading to complete enlightenment. Learning to die a natural, meaningful death is one of the most useful things we can do in our lives right now. If we know the correct way to die, we can go straight to liberation.

—— *FOUR* ——
EMPTINESS

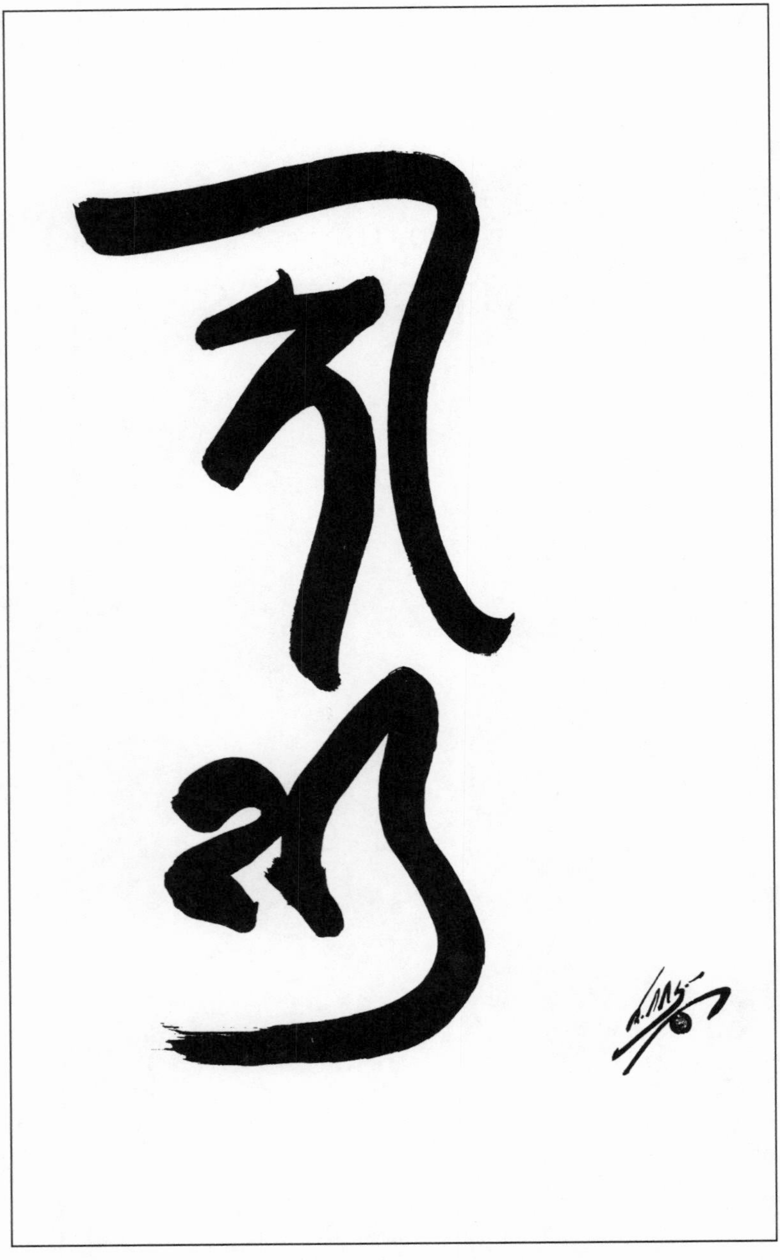

T HE PRINCIPLE OF EMPTINESS IS IN ALL THE
teachings of the Buddha. He placed specific emphasis on
emptiness in the last teachings he gave, which are called the Second and Third Turnings of the Wheel of Dharma. In those teachings, the Buddha expounded the concept of emptiness, but of
these two teachings, the Second Turning of the Wheel of
Dharma particularly concerns the teaching on emptiness and
wisdom. Much of this teaching is found in the *Prajnaparamita-
sutra,* which the Buddha taught at the request of his bodhisattva
disciples.

The first time Lord Buddha "turned the wheel of Dharma,"
he taught the Four Noble Truths. The second time, he taught
about emptiness. The third time, he taught about buddha nature. That is how the Buddha himself described the progression
of his teachings.

The great master Nagarjuna explains the three turns of the
wheel of Dharma in his own way. Nagarjuna is one of the eight
great Indian masters in Buddhist history, sometimes called the
Eight Great Ornaments of the Earth. He says that in the first
turn of the wheel, Lord Buddha taught about the self. At the
second turn of the wheel, Lord Buddha taught about emptiness
of the self. And third, Lord Buddha taught about clarifying all
the consequences of the first and second teachings. That is how
Nagarjuna describes the teachings.

The great master Aryadeva, another one of the Eight Great
Ornaments of the Earth, also describes the three turns of the

wheel of Dharma. He maintains that the first teaching was given to guide the disciples away from accumulating bad or negative karma. In the second teaching Lord Buddha taught how to overcome the self, the source of all defilements. This teaching is the teaching on emptiness. The third turn of the wheel, according to Aryadeva, was the teaching on how to overcome views and philosophies that limit perfect, accurate understanding.

The essence of the Three Turnings of the Wheel of Dharma is simplicity. It is where Buddhism started. It is where we must look whenever we trace any teachings of Lord Buddha. That is why the greatest Buddhist masters wrote commentaries about it, and why all followers of this path to enlightenment must contemplate these teachings and practice them. The subject of emptiness in these three teachings comprises seventeen major sutras that are collectively entitled the *Prajnaparamita-sutra*. Different collections may group them differently, so the number of books may vary, but these words of the Buddha are the source of the teaching on emptiness. All the other sutras touch on it, but these seventeen are quite specific.

The first of the seventeen *Prajnaparamita* sutras is one of the longest. The Tibetan-language version, translated from Sanskrit, consists of 400,000 sentences which make up 100,000 *shlokas*, or four-line verses. It is printed as twelve volumes, and each volume is 800 to 1,000 pages. One of the smallest of the seventeen is the *Heart Sutra,* which can be translated into a paragraph in English. The shortest of all consists of one syllable, the syllable "ah" (In Tibetan it is the "small ah." It is the "one-letter sutra" or *shechen yige chik pa.*) The main theme of all these sutras, from the longest *Prajnaparamita* sutra to the shortest, is emptiness. The *Prajnaparamita* sutras discuss emptiness in detail.

Emptiness is described as the basis that makes anything possible. Everything is a manifestation of interdependence, and everything is emptiness. That is emptiness summed up in one paradoxical sentence. We must try to understand this. Everything exists, but all things exist as an interdependent manifestations. We have seen these interdependent phenomena in connection with reincarnation. The twelve links of interdependence outline the interdependent nature of what we call existence. If we look beyond the interdependent manifestation, we will see that there is no independent existence. That is emptiness. It may also be stated that there is nothing that is not interrelated, therefore there is nothing that is not emptiness.

Many people are confused about emptiness, but it is not such a difficult subject when seen from the point of view of figure and ground. Emptiness is the ground, and interdependent manifestation, samsara, is the figure imposed on the ground. In this way, emptiness becomes the reason why anything is possible. It is the ground or space on which anything might be created, and is created: it makes the existence of samsara possible, and the attainment of enlightenment possible. The improvement of sentient beings is possible because of emptiness, and so is the activity of buddhas and bodhisattvas. Because everything is interdependent, when all the conditions are correct, anything can happen. Emptiness makes it possible for a sentient being who is suffering in samsara to also be a buddha by nature. When that being purifies the relative samsaric obscuration that binds it, then it is possible for it to become enlightened. None of this could be done without emptiness. If everything in existence were substantial and permanent, no one could grow old or learn anything; nothing could change, either for better or for worse; nothing could be improved, because there would be no room for it. This is common sense if you see emptiness simply. Emptiness provides the questions and the answers to all the questions, because it allows for movement and change. It allows for insight and realization.

In one sutra Lord Buddha taught about emptiness by saying that no phenomena, internal or external—external such as elements, or internal such as thoughts—have solid existence. Nothing has. Nothing is substantial. Then he went on to say that birth is emptiness; he enumerated all phenomena, all of which are emptiness; and finally he said death is emptiness. From the germination of a tree from the seed, to the death of the tree and its total disintegration when each element—fire, water, earth, and air—returns to the universal elements, everything is emptiness. At the end of his dissertation, he said that everything is a miracle, a miracle of interdependence of all causes and conditions. When all the causes and conditions are in perfect harmony, a miracle results.

Look at a beautiful flower and try to see how this is possible. It is a miracle of interdependent manifestation. Think about it. A flower is possible because of emptiness. It germinates from seed, puts forth shoots, and grows into an adult plant that produces a bud, which unfurls into a rose. When the petals drop off and the plant shrivels into a brown, dead stem, it returns back into the emptiness from whence it came, before it was a seed. Everything is emptiness, therefore everything is the miraculous display of interdependent origination, cause and condition.

There are several ways to view emptiness. There is the practical view, and there is a more spiritual view. Concerning the ordinary view of emptiness, the Buddha said that nothing is happening, therefore everything is happening. It is easy to use ourselves as examples of the ordinary viewpoint. A human family may be more or less happy and stable, but it also can at times have a crisis. In either situation, the husband, wife, and children are all the same people, in the same environment. Nothing has changed except that there may be a communication breakdown among family members. It is the same family, however, living in a two-bedroom house with a garden, with the children going to school every day and the parents going to work. So nothing has really changed, and nothing is happening on one level, but on another level everything is happening because causes and conditions have created lack of communication, the manifestation of which is a problem. Relatively, emptiness is filled with situations that take place against the backdrop of emptiness, that arise out of emptiness, where ultimately nothing is happening. Everything in relative reality happens only as an interdependent manifestation within the ultimate realm of emptiness.

The Buddha also taught about the interrelationship between external existence and the internal processes of individual sentient beings. This also derives from emptiness. In the sutras, and particularly in the Abhidharma teachings, this is explained in clear and practical terms. We relate to the external world through our senses, which are focused in our bodies: the eyes see, the ears hear, the nose smells. Our sense reactions when we touch a particular thing depend completely on the causes and conditions that created our body in that lifetime, causes and conditions that are the result of the twelve interdependent links. The manner in which that external factor manifests is also due to causes and conditions. The Buddha explains that our perception of the human beings of this planet, earth, does not apply to the entire human realm, but only to phenomena for human beings of this planet. Phenomena in another place might appear much different, but we can have no clear concept of that, really, since we know the human realm only as we experience it here.

The Buddha gives a hypothetical example: if your mind could enter another human being—the person right next to you, for instance—and relate to the environment through that person, you would find that the same environment of which you were previously aware becomes different, according to the perceptions of the other person. Every individual perceives things differently through the senses. Not only that, in one lifetime, from childhood to adulthood and the different stages of aging, the ways an individual relates to life and environment continually change. People who have reached their forties do not have the same expectations, desires, or attitudes as they did in their thirties, or in their twenties. So differences of perception occur even within the life of one person. These are all external environmental factors that are physical, emotional, and mental.

Why is this so? Emptiness. The Buddha gives another example that is a bit more spiritual, the example of the River Ganges, the holiest river in India. He said that if a human being in India goes to the Ganges, to that being it is a holy river, and to bathe in it is to be blessed. If the being who goes to the river is an animal, the river is a pleasant source of water for drinking and bathing. But to a hungry ghost, the river is something to run away from. A hungry ghost cannot drink or even touch it without great pain. To a hell-being, the Ganges will resemble flowing lava that burns. So even a holy river, encountered by beings of the different realms, is not the same river. This is because of emptiness, from which causes and conditions arise and play themselves out.

All beings of the six realms experience the same river in different ways because beings from separate realms have different karma, while those from the same realm have similar karma. A particular term is given for this in Abhidharma; in Tibetan it is *kal nyum*. *Kal* relates to the time, or timing, and *nyum* means equal, thus "equal timing." Karmic causes and conditions make all human beings see, hear, and be affected by things in a similar way. We are all in a similar condition and have a common ground of perception, despite individual differences. Some people reading this may think the information is valuable. Some may think, "I already know that." Some may think, "This fellow doesn't make much sense." Someone may wonder, "Does he know what he's talking about?" Regardless of divergent opinions, we all still have a common ground, which is *kal nyum*. It is almost impossible for us to be exactly the same. There is an infinite variety of appearances, thoughts, and feelings—all because of emptiness. We would all look the same if it were not for emptiness. This is an explanation of emptiness from an ordinary standpoint.

Regarding the more spiritual aspect of emptiness, the Buddha said that although every sentient being has buddha nature, each can still suffer in samsara because of emptiness. He goes on to say that even the most ignorant sentient being can attain enlightenment because of emptiness. It might take billions of lifetimes from the time one makes the decision to attain enlightenment until it is actually attained, but when it is, those billions of lifetimes become less than a moment, because of emptiness. Mothers often say they can hardly recall the pain of childbirth once they hold their newborn child in their arms.

The Buddha taught that the compassion of the buddhas and the devotion of sentient beings can meet, because of emptiness. Although the buddhas have compassion, if a sentient being does not have devotion, his or her compassion will not be effective. Why? Because of emptiness. Like everything else, compassion and devotion are phenomena based on emptiness. Also, devotion predisposes sentient beings to receive and profit from compassion. A buddha or bodhisattva cannot force a sentient being into buddhahood. The sutra goes on in this vein, repeating different examples, but the point may be summed up by saying that all the delusions, obscurations, and defilements are emptiness— just as all knowledge, all wisdom, and all compassion are emptiness.

It would be helpful to consider some of the sound advice and warnings given in the texts. If we understand that ignorance and defilements are emptiness, and that wisdom and positive qualities are emptiness, then we might tend to develop an attitude that everything is emptiness, and so what does it matter how we behave? We might feel it is OK to do whatever we feel like doing, since everything is emptiness anyway. One of the gravest warnings in the teachings of the Buddha is against such an attitude. The particular expression used in Tibetan is very descriptive: *Tong nyi dar long*. *Tong nyi* means emptiness, and *dar long* means to stand up as an enemy. Knowing emptiness becomes an enemy of progress if a person's attitude becomes careless and irresponsible. It is definitely a wrong view.

There is another warning in the Tantras. In Tibetan it is precisely said, *Tong pa nyi la nye na ta nyi na sherab chung nam pung war jur.* This means that one who has limited wisdom and perceives emptiness wrongly will be destroyed. That is, the person's life will become useless, and he or she will fall back, perhaps becoming a source of wrong view for others, which makes the person's situation even worse. Understanding emptiness halfway is not good enough. Misunderstanding can create great damage.

The correct approach is stated in a well-known Tibetan saying, "Your view may be limitless as the sky, like space, but your mindfulness, awareness, and actions should be as fine as powder." This means that however much you may know about emptiness, that much you have to be mindful, aware, and disciplined in your actions. So, if you know emptiness, and with that knowledge you practice discipline and methods of mind training, much benefit is there, because you will be engaged in constructive, positive activity and will not become fanatically disciplined. You will not become obsessed with attachment to your particular method, because you know it is just a method. You will be on the alert, monitoring yourself. You will know negativity is not a solid thing. It is empty. And you will know that a positive thing is also not substantial. It is empty. However, you still work with positive methods to overcome negativity. Working like this, understanding emptiness becomes a very effective practice.

Emptiness and interdependent manifestation are closely related, and the easiest way to explain and understand emptiness is in terms of the interdependent links of origination. That is the samsaric pattern, already discussed, which outlines how and why sentient beings evolve and continue, lifetime after lifetime. There is another pattern that is like enlightenment, the interdependence of enlightenment. This is how a buddha manifests and benefits human beings. The normal samsaric interdependence consists of the twelve links: ignorance, impulse to act, impulse to consciousness, consciousness, sense perception, contact, pleasure and pain, attachment, grasping, becoming, birth, and death. These links bind us. Until the enlightenment of buddhahood, all the processes are interdependent. That is not difficult to understand.

As an individual, Prince Siddhartha, when he attained enlightenment, went beyond interdependent influence, but his manifestation was not beyond it. His manifestation was totally related to interdependence. Those who had the karma to see him when he was in a physical body were present 2,5000 years ago. Those who have karma to see him now, see him in different forms. Those who have karma to receive his blessing in a direct way will receive it. Those who have the karma to receive his blessing only in an indirect way, that is the only way for them. It is not a situation where the Buddha's blessing is equal for everyone, and everyone must receive equally. That doesn't happen, because everyone has different capacities to receive blessings according to individual causes and conditions. The potential to receive the blessing in full is there for every being, as is buddha nature, but the ability to receive it may be blocked in varying degrees, just as our realization of our own buddha nature is blocked. An often-quoted Tibetan proverb is that the nectar of Dharma might rain for one hundred thousand years, but a pot turned upside-down will remain empty.

Followers of the Buddha still pray for the liberation of all sentient beings. Although the Buddha attained enlightenment 2,500 years ago, there are still many sentient beings who are suffering. Even many of the Buddha's own disciples are still in deep confusion. We can't go and say to the Buddha, "You dropped the ball," because the problem is ours. It is our play. The Buddha, as an individual, is free from all the interdependent influences, but his manifestation is not. His manifestation is an interdependent manifestation, although it is not an ordinary one bound by samsara. There are suffering beings who have a karmic link with him, and because of his dedication to liberate beings who exist in an interdependent relative reality, his manifestation also exists there. Although the Buddha may not be inhabiting a *nirmanakaya* form as he did when he taught on earth, the presence of the Buddha is in every contact that inspires and encourages our practice or gives us insight into the nature of mind.

This is one of the ways the practice of devotion works. We have to develop compassion in order to develop pure devotion, and vice versa. The purity of our devotion to the Buddha determines the purity of the blessing we can receive. If we want to see something clearly, we have to have good eyes. The better our eyes are, the clearer our vision will be. The purer our devotion, the purer the blessing, and the more we are able to benefit. Those who don't have such pure devotion and pure compassion need advice and practice to establish those qualities. The potential for pure devotion is within each of us, but if we don't do anything about it, it will not just come out by itself. Even if it were to come out by accident, it will quickly be lost without the foundation to support and nurture it, like a seed that sprouts accidentally in a corner of the driveway and quickly dies because there is not adequate soil or water there.

This is mentioned in the *Bodhisattvacharyavatara* of the great master Shantideva. He said that in the darkest night, the split second of lightning is brighter than anything on earth, but then it's gone. By accident, we can have some kind of pure encounter with our real ultimate potential, but that is not something we can keep up. In times of difficulty, when something extremely shocking or painful happens, there may come a moment of insight, or vision, or a glimpse of recognition of something other than the ordinary. But as soon as things settle down, it's over. It doesn't last. Instant enlightenment happens after a lot of work. We have to have discipline and practice the methods to establish a foundation for it.

APPLICATION AND PRACTICE OF EMPTINESS

In both the Sutras and the Tantras, Lord Buddha guided his disciples in the application of the understanding of emptiness. The teachings on emptiness are often taken as an intellectual, theoretical exercise. Of course, that is correct in one way, but the points described in the Sutras and Tantras go much deeper than that. There emptiness is defined as the essence of all things. It was through his teachings on emptiness that the Buddha introduced his disciples to the nature of phenomena. He also taught how to practice the understanding of emptiness and how to bring the knowledge and understanding of emptiness into everyday life through meditation, prayer, recitation, and all forms of activity.

The universal condition gives us guidelines for the practice and application of emptiness. Sentient beings have different levels of inner attainment, which, for practical purposes, are categorized into higher realms and lower realms. There are three higher realms, including heaven, and three lower realms, including hell. These are different levels of mind that manifest in different levels of form.

The causes and conditions of each of the six realms are six kinds of defilements. A human being can experience the defilements of all realms. For instance, the defilement or poison of anger is intensified in the hell realm. Yet a human can be overwhelmed by anger, and it can make everything in life unpleasant. No matter how nice the environment is, an angry person will not notice it, because anger has caused it to be perceived as antagonistic. And angry person may become physically ill, feel aggressive, or feel like killing someone, smashing something, screaming—the anger can get completely out of hand. When a person is overwhelmed by ignorance, characteristic of the animal realm, perception is clouded. This is the case no matter how much the person might know, and despite academic credentials. You feel as if you don't know anything, and maybe you are even confused about who you are. When we are inflated by pride, we might feel as if we are gods, better than everyone else, even above normal and proper modes of conduct. Of course, the problem with the god realm is that although pleasure may be experienced for eons, the sudden decline and fall at the end is terrible, and it is followed by rebirth in hell. When taken over by jealousy, we experience in the human realm the conflicts of the *asuras,* or jealous demi-gods, and are never able to rest. When we are beset by attachment and desire, we experience the defilements of *pretas,* or hungry ghosts. Hatred creates for us our own private hell realm, destroying peace of mind and happiness. In each of the six realms of birth, then, a characteristic defilement is intensified. The defilement becomes the cause and condition for an individual to take birth in the particular realm associated with that defilement. Human birth is the best springboard to enlightenment because humans have the opportunity to experience, balance, and transcend defilements of all realms.

The Buddha said, in Abhidharma and some of the sutras on karma, that whether a being is human, animal, or other, the six realms are not limited to the physical condition of any particular location or particular environment. When we look at our planet of birth, we see many peoples with many different characteristics—Africans, Europeans, Asians of India, Russia, China, and Tibet. On planets in neighboring solar systems, the inhabitants would most likely be more different from us than the varieties we see on this planet are different from each other. Different combinations of elements might make them unrecognizable as human beings to people of this planet. Buddha taught about different planets, galaxies, and solar systems in Abhidharma. It is very clear in the Tripitaka and the Sutras as well. But in the Tantras, Buddha gave additional details.

He said that other human beings—that is, beings having the same level of mind as we do—can have totally different physical conditions. If they were to come here, what we can pass through as air might be a wall to them, while they might easily go through what is a wall to us. He gave a clear explanation that some human beings have drastically different operating principles and will not experience phenomena in exactly the same way we experience them. For them form is emptiness, eye is emptiness, ear is emptiness, sound is emptiness, touch is emptiness, body is emptiness, and this can go on and on. One of the reasons for describing all this is to explain emptiness. Emptiness is in all realms, even realms that manifest far apart and in widely different ways. Human beings who might seem strange to us are not more enlightened than we are, nor are we more enlightened than they; because of the physical condition, everything that is relevant to us can be totally irrelevant to beings manifesting differently. Emptiness is a universal principle. It is not only something that belongs to 2,500 years of history. It is not a new discovery. It is a truth of the universe. It is emptiness.

When you have a clear and practical understanding of emptiness, it naturally and effortlessly becomes the key for handling any situation. Knowing emptiness, you will not view any particular problem as solid and unchangeable. You will not be overwhelmed by a good situation and forget your principles. Neither can circumstances overwhelm you to the point of destroying you. You know it is all manifestation of causes and conditions in the space of emptiness. That is all. Conditions are right for good fortune, so you are happy, or conditions are negative, so there are problems. It is as simple as that. This way you don't become neurotic. You don't become completely materialistic. You are able to lead a balanced life, one that includes spiritual and material processes, meditation, and prayer, as well as mundane activities. You will be able to face everything without being affected negatively. When individuals understand emptiness, life goes more smoothly. It is completely natural.

All the most esoteric philosophical teachings in Vajrayana Buddhism are based on the idea of emptiness. These appear in Vinaya, Abhidharma, the Sutras, and the Tantras, and are tremendously profound. Two of these important philosophical definitions are *rangtong* and *jentong*. Translation of these two terms is extremely difficult because they are not ordinary terminology but part of a specialized philosophical language. *Rangtong* may be roughly translated as "internal emptiness" or "self-emptiness." *Jentong* is "external emptiness" or "emptiness outside." These are rough translations, but close to the meaning.

The *rangtong* and *jentong* views look at the same subject from a different angle. A simple example is a coastline, where the water meets the land. It may be reached in two ways. The shore may be reached from the ocean by boat; or by land, on foot or in some vehicle. *Rangtong* and *jentong* are like that, reaching the same end from different directions.

Rangtong and *jentong* can be applied to any subject, but here it might be more meaningful to use them to view buddha nature. From the *rangtong* "self-emptiness" view, the philosophical definition of the perfect buddha nature is that it is absolutely empty of dualistic existence. The buddha nature is perfect, beyond dualistic identity. The *jentong* "external emptiness" view is that perfect buddha nature is free from any kind of relative solid existence. Based on the general understanding of emptiness and the combination of *rangtong* and *jentong*, great masters have integrated both views. There have also been masters who were proponents of the *jentong* view or the *rangtong* view only, and who held it very strongly. Either way, the conclusion is the same.

There is a way to take emptiness from this esoteric, philosophical dimension and bring it into Buddhist practice, applying it in ordinary life. A Buddhist starts by what is called taking refuge. This means having confidence and taking instruction from places and persons capable of actually providing refuge: the time-tested teachings of the Buddha in the texts, the realized teachers whose guidance is necessary, and our sincere companions on the path. The historical Buddha, the Dharma—the texts or teachings—and the Sangha—the guide, teacher, or spiritual friend—are the sources of refuge. This should be understood and respected. As a condition of life, the disciple can practice Dharma under the advice of a teacher with the blessing of the Buddha, but the final refuge is enlightenment. Because of this, we do not look at the historical Buddha, the teachings, or the guides as permanent, substantial entities. When we understand that the Buddha, the Dharma, and our spiritual friends are necessary but impermanent means on the path to enlightenment, we apply the principle of emptiness in taking refuge. These objects of refuge are the conditions for the practice of Dharma, and all practitioners need their help. With their blessing and their advice, it is possible to be successful in Dharma practice to the point of eventually becoming buddha. This is the application of emptiness in the refuge.

The second application of emptiness is in prayers and meditation. The fundamental devotional prayer and the fundamental meditation, such as *shinay*—"calming the mind"—provide an experience of emptiness. When you pray with pure devotion, this perfect feeling of mind clarifies all the suffering and all the delusions while you are praying. During the prayer recited with pure devotion, you feel perfectly pure. Of course, in the beginning, when you stop the prayer, the problems come back. That's normal. But while you are praying, you feel blessed.

The same is true with the basic meditation practice. When you practice *shinay,* for example, you are in the quietest state of mind; everything is perfect. Everything becomes pure. And of course, for beginners, when meditation stops and daily activity starts, then that perfect feeling goes away. Prayer and meditation, done properly, can give a glimpse of the experience of emptiness.

The third application of emptiness is when bodhichitta is practiced. It is the essence of Sutra teachings. With the development of compassion, loving-kindness, and joy, the practitioner can appreciate anything, happiness or suffering. The value of each is understood. In one sutra the Buddha said that the one who has bodhichitta, even if he is suffering, he suffers happily. The alchemy of transforming negativity within you and within others is developing bodhichitta. Because of bodhichitta, everything becomes perfect. Positive and negative situations alike become the perfect conditions in which to practice bodhichitta. That is how fundamental bodhisattva practice is an application of emptiness.

The fourth method of applying emptiness in practice is the essence of Tantra. This involves the fundamental understanding that every sentient being is buddha by nature, that every environment is Pure Land by nature. Until one recognizes this, one remains in samsara. When one does recognize it, that is enlightenment. Samsara, when its nature is not recognized, causes suffering. But when its nature is recognized, it causes enlightenment. This recognition happens through your practice. The practice of discipline, the practice of compassion, the practice of morality, and so forth, are the means through which you recognize the essential nature of phenomenal existence.

When the essence of buddha is recognized, it is the final moment. The time in samsara of an enlightened buddha, relatively, could have been billions of centuries in billions of different samsaric realms before reaching buddhahood, but in the ultimate sense, it is not even one second of uncounted time. That is the ultimate level of emptiness. Although as ordinary beings we cannot truly understand this, and it cannot be described, in our own experiences there is an analogous situation. Think about a time you have had an operation, dental work, or an accident in which you were injured, when you think the pain will never stop. Time becomes so long that even though it may only be a few minutes of intense pain, it seems like hours. Then suddenly the pain stops, and it's over. That is a sweet and wonderful moment, as if the pain never was. It is almost forgotten. This is not anything like enlightenment, but it gives an idea of emptiness as experienced in time, an idea of what the countless rebirths and seemingly endless suffering becomes in the last moment before enlightenment.

This description of these four applications of emptiness are very brief and rough, but it is a simple way to see how emptiness is used at different levels of Buddhist practice. We should be able to pray, meditate, do good works, avoid negative activities, try to help others, develop devotion, and develop compassion, but never should we maintain the idea and concept that any of it is real or substantial. We practice these things as a spontaneous manifestation of the perfect buddha nature inside. We are merely facilitating sentient beings' positive conditions when we help them. When we practice Dharma, we facilitate the awakening of our buddha nature, doing everything possible to assist that process. If we hold on to good action as if it were solid, we become neurotic.

A person who has a good working understanding of emptiness is not only able to live his or her life more effectively and meaningfully, but is also able to share this knowledge with others. All people can benefit from the application of emptiness, not only Buddhists. When a person is dying, for instance, it is very helpful to understand emptiness. We all know people who have died or are dying. Many young people these days have friends who are dying of AIDS or other diseases, or they may have a serious disease themselves. Although it is a difficult and painful thing, it is also a great opportunity.

Tibetans have many sayings. An appropriate one is found in an epic tale about the heroic deeds of a king and his trusted soldiers. There is one very good line, spoken during a terribly painful scene on a battlefield: "No matter what happens to my body, it is only my body that is hurt. No one can hurt my mind." Just because body and mind are interrelated, it does not follow that if body suffers, mind suffers too. Our mind does not have to suffer. If there is a clear understanding of emptiness, much physical suffering can be alleviated. When the insubstantiality of a phenomenon like pain is recognized, it is possible to go beyond it.

There is another saying, this time from the Buddha. It is about how to deal with defilements like anger. It may be paraphrased as follows. When you are angry, if you are able, just look at the face of the anger. Sit, look, and ask, "What is it?" Maybe you are furious enough to want to be violent, but instead of doing that just sit and ask, "What is it? Where is it?" Suddenly you will realize that the anger is not there. Your anger is only a reaction, a result, of several interdependent manifestations. That is all it is. This can be applied to any negative state of mind, like attachment, desire, jealousy—anything.

Habit is also a factor to be dealt with. The Tibetan term is *pa cha che dipa*. Defilement is also, of course, habit, but it is a little bit different. *Pa cha che dipa* is a very subtle obstacle. An example is the way we project our own thoughts, feelings, or motivations on others. This can be very difficult to see and overcome, and it takes effort to do so. When we always find ourselves making the same mistake by misunderstanding others and judging them in an inaccurate, stupid, or uncompassionate way, we are being blocked by this habitual pattern. Later we find out that we were wrong, but usually by then it's too late, the damage is done. We can only learn from the mistake. These are subtle habitual obstacles stemming directly from the concept of "I."

Westerners often seem to have a problem with self-worth. Many people say they hate themselves, or don't like themselves. They are sure they are no good. This is probably because they do not understand the fact of buddha nature. Understanding buddha nature is the best means of overcoming this low self-esteem, but in addition to that is the practice of emptiness. From the emptiness point of view, the person who is hated, the self, is not there. And even if disagreeable traits are there, because of emptiness it is always possible to improve. There are no permanent hateful states. Emptiness is, in a way, like the Philosopher's Stone that Western alchemists once searched for. It is there, but not there; it is the essence of everything; it is the question and the answer to all questions. That is emptiness.

———*FIVE*———
TANTRIC SCIENCE

TANTRIC SCIENCE IS VERY HARD TO DEFINE.
Tantric science, from one point of view, encompasses everything. From another point of view, science can only be activity that employs the scientific method. It is a commonly held opinion that Buddhism is the most scientific religion. The reason for this is that in Buddhism an answer can be found for everything, both worldly and spiritual phenomena. Buddha encouraged his followers to question and to test. He said that you must ask questions if you have doubts. This is true according to Buddhism, but it is not necessary to take my word for it. It is better to find out for yourself, by asking questions and exploring on your own. The emphasis on validating truth is one reason Buddhism can be considered scientific. There are others. Tibetan Buddhism teaches about the profound sciences of life, all links to the path toward realization. There are ten aspects of knowledge, five ordinary and five extraordinary. Tantric sciences number among the five extraordinary aspects of knowledge. The Tantric sciences are medicine, mathematics, and astrology. All have the highest purpose of benefiting others.

Science appears in the Sutras and the Tantras. The teaching of the Buddha, as a whole, is scientific teaching. It is well ordered and systematic, and not limited to Tantra. In Tantra, however, there is specific emphasis and detail that makes the subjects under consideration very clear. The name Tantric science is an appropriate title for that reason. Science, in the Buddhist sense, means the principles are taught clearly, with detailed explana-

Unity of two truths is the foundation of correctness

tions to answer any questions that might come up. Nothing is to be taken on faith. There is a valid and complete connection with reality, the truth of which can be tested. Buddha taught for more than forty-five years after his enlightenment, and every teaching is scientific.

Often people, even those with a Buddhist background and from the East, are quite ignorant about this. Because of lack of information or understanding, people believe that Buddhism is not scientific. That is like saying the sun is not warm. It is very important for all Buddhists to acknowledge and understand the scientific nature of the Dharma. Many people whose origins are Buddhist respect the discoveries of scientists much more than the words of the Buddha. Yet many scientists respect the teaching of Buddha. In the writings of scientist Albert Einstein one can find reflections of Buddhist thought. The theory of relativity unquestionably embodies the Buddhist view. It is a good thing for Buddhist people, who are fortunate to be born in this family of Buddhism, to learn about the practical value of their religion.

The scope of Tantric science is enormous, and a brief chapter can only touch on a few aspects of it. It ranges from the science of understanding and working with the mind and its subtleties to elemental physical science. Physical science is itself a vast subject, but we may understand it better by relating it to the physical body of a human being and to our planet. Buddha taught about the physical science of human beings many times. He taught about it in Abhidharma and in many sutras. It is also in almost all the major tantras. The four categories of the Buddha's teaching—Vinaya, Abhidharma, the Sutras, and the Tantras—all contain teachings about physical science. Abhidharma gives the simplest explication; the discussion in the Sutras is more advanced. Buddha taught the final details in Tantra, which answers the last questions. So there is the fundamental teaching, the advanced teaching, and the completion of the subject. Buddha taught, in all three phases, that the human body is the immediate, personal home of the mind. That is how he described it. Without the mind, the body is a dead body. No matter how good a condition the body is in, without mind, it is dead. It is only alive when the mind joins it, lives and functions through it.

The physical body is divided into groupings of organs: the five major internal organs, such as the heart; and the six major containers inside the body, such as the stomach. Through these the complex structure of bones, nerves, circulatory system, and so forth work together with three balancing substances. These substances translate as bile, described as yellow; phlegm, described as white; and air, which provides pressure for movement inside the body. When these elements balance, we have good health. When they are out of balance, we become ill. These factors affect us both physically and mentally.

The body, when all systems balance, is a good home for the mind. There is another, more refined system that relates to mental health, which functions within the outer physical system just described. This system consists of subtle channels through which vital force and the physical essence flow. The energy and essence work together in the central channel and smaller channels that radiate from it, controlling the functions of the subtle body.

All this begins, as we have seen, when the mind enters the first-stage liquid body, accompanied by the energy essence, as happens whenever conception of a living being takes place. The karmic forces of our past lives motivate this process. Because of desire, anger, ignorance, and other defilements, we have generated the causes for rebirth. This is the beginning of biological science in Buddhism, when, due to karmic force, the causes take on material form and power. The liquid body, the subtle essence of the mind, and the karmic force—all three together—are the beginning of a living being. With this power and form the channels are developed. As the channels develop, the energy flows along them. When enough channels and adequate physical structures to go with them develop, a child is born. More channels develop as we grow from newborn child to adulthood. The channels stop developing when the body is physically mature. As the body grows older, the channels are affected by age.

There are three main channels inside the body, one in the middle, one to the right, and one to the left. The right channel has ten major branches, and the left has fourteen major branches. There are five branches in the direction of the heart known as the five secret branches, which are very important. There are thirty-two channels including the major three trunks. From these thirty-two are formed six major stations or energy centers. One is the crown, above the top of the head; the next is on the top of the head; the third is the throat, the fourth is the heart, the fifth is the navel, and the sixth is below the navel. Out of each station, branches extend throughout the body, to every last pore. The number of branches is very clearly noted in the Tantric texts. These things are not necessary to know at this stage because we cannot do very much with the information. It is merely to give an idea of what is involved.

There are also five major classifications of energy forces that help the body function. The first is disposal or elimination energy. It is the force that helps dispose of waste, causing hair and nails to grow, dead cells to be shed, perspiration, and other types of elimination. The second force holds things together, as water holds clay together and assists the earth element to maintain a specific shape. The third energy force is heat. It is very important for digestion and keeping everything functioning and alive. It helps keep the body sound and free from deterioration. Pressure is the fourth energy force. It is a powerful aspect of energy. It might even be called antigravity. It is what ensures that our brain is supplied with blood, even if we are standing; if we stand on our heads, blood still circulates to our feet. The last one of the five is called "all-pervasive," balancer or distributor. It helps move the essential things to all parts of the body at the right time and in the right quantities.

Similar to the five major energy forces are the major types of air, which have a close relationship to physical breath. Combinations of air act throughout the channels, reaching to their finest ends, bringing nourishment of various kinds to the smallest physical component. Every single pore breathes. Meditation that makes use of breathing and correct physical posture is recommended in Tantric science for healing certain kinds of mental disturbances. The five airs and the meditation posture, considered together, give an idea of how Tantric science works in a way that we can all experience with practice.

When meditation is taught, the first thing introduced is the proper way to sit. Correct posture assists the flow of energy throughout the channels. Sitting in the right position is the first step to balance the mind. The virtue of sitting properly when you meditate cannot be overemphasized. When posture is taught for meditation, it is usually described in terms of seven points, but for this particular purpose five points of posture are given for meditation.

The breathing of air, which assists the circulation of energy, is divided into five aspects to correspond with the five aspects of air. The air always has to be renewed, so that breathing is a continual rejuvenation process, or at least it should be when done correctly. Air is like the other nutrients our body requires. We must draw it from the universe constantly.

The correct sitting posture is cross-legged on a mat or cushion on the floor. Hands lie together in the lap, the back is straight, and the neck should be slightly bent. The eyes are neither wide open nor closed, but semi-opened. Some Buddha statues show the eyes in this way. These are the five positions of the physical body that make up the correct meditation posture.

The five airs resemble the five energies. The first air is the air of elimination and disposal, which assists this process throughout the body. When we sit in the cross-legged position, this air for elimination becomes centralized.

The second air is described as water air. Putting the hands together, right hand above left, and just resting them on the lap assists the function of this type of air, which keeps all the other airs functioning together. It is like the water that holds the particles of earth together in a clay figure. The five airs are held together in a similar way, and keeping the hands together centralizes the water air and helps balance it.

The third postural point is sitting with the back straight, which is designed to centralize the earth air. The earth air is a stabilizing air, a kind of foundation for all the other types of air. It is a solid aspect of air. When your back is straight, this air is more easily balanced. Keeping the arms straight also assists this air.

The fire air keeps the body warm and maintains the body so that it remains fresh and does not disintegrate. As soon as we die, that air departs and the body disintegrates. The fire air also has the power to circulate substances throughout the body. Keeping the neck slightly bent supports the action of this air by centralizing it.

The airy type of air is movement. It makes movement throughout the body possible. The position with eyes half-shut and also with the tongue gently touching the upper palate centralizes the airy air. When correct sitting posture is assumed, all the five types of air become balanced according to the structure and function of each part of the body. Presented like this, it might seem mysterious, but in certain tantras—the *Hevajra-tantra*, for instance—these things are clearly written down in the texts, with complete explanations.

Confusion, neurosis, and serious mental disturbance come

from an imbalance of these five energies or five airs. There is a correspondence of these energies and airs with the defilements of jealousy, anger, ignorance, attachment, and pride. The disposal air is related to jealousy, water air is related to anger, earth air relates to ignorance, fire air relates to attachment or desire, and airy air relates to pride, or ego. All ordinary sentient beings have these defilements to a greater or lesser extent, and we work to keep them in balance.

Tantric science provides specific techniques for keeping the defilements in balance so they can become tools for achieving realization rather than generators of more negativity. Meditation on the breath in the correct posture is one example of such a technique. Keeping the defilements in balance allows us to maintain our mental and physical balance. Until enlightenment we will have to contend with the defilements, so knowing methods to balance them is crucial to our progress. When any one of the defilements gains ascendancy, we suffer for it. Imbalances can have mild to severe effects. We may be temporarily confused, chronically neurotic, or seriously ill mentally. To be able to sit down in a beneficial posture for a period of time prepares us to calm the mind through meditation. It is the first step in maintaining or regaining mental health.

Essential substance can be divided into two categories. The first is the pure universal essence, and the second is the essence derived from what we eat, drink, and breathe. The universal essence is the most important component of our physical systems, for which the essence of our environmental nourishment is a reinforcement. Essential substance keeps all the senses functioning. Each sense has a particular essence that nourishes it. The eye has its own essence, called *lung po* in Tibetan. The eyeball is the focus of that essence. The essences of food, air, and water can make the parts of our physical bodies to which the specific nutrient is particularly related strong and healthy. According to the Tantra, if we eat something good, after seven days the essence of that food becomes part of us. This is how the plants, minerals, and animals of the earth may be used for healing.

There is an intensive method of purification of environmental factors, *tsalung,* as well as a meditation technique to assist in removal of current obstacles. It is an important and powerful practice, but it is not taught casually because it is quite dangerous. It is dangerous because it is extremely effective. It is also sacred. If everything is done right, wisdom is naturally developed, because all conditions through which the mind functions—that is, the body—become free of obstacles. That way wisdom is developed. If it is done wrongly, however, it can be seriously disabling, and the individual will no longer be able to function normally. Getting it right is not easy, either. A foundation of disciplined practice and a depth of understanding must be attained before attempting such advanced methods.

Otherwise, it would be as if you need to have electrical repairs done but are not a qualified electrician. You try to fix them anyway, but you confuse the wires, so when you turn on the light switch in the living room the kitchen light goes on, or you turn on the kitchen light and the air conditioner starts up. You may damage things. You might even electrocute yourself. The body functions in a very subtle way, and if you do specialized exercises without proper guidance, motivation, and 100 percent knowledge and understanding, you will find yourself in deep trouble. If you get one thing wrong, everything goes wrong. The first thing that can be guaranteed is that you will go crazy. And you wouldn't even know it, because you would have such a big ego you would think you were perfectly OK. Everyone you meet would think you were crazy, but you would think *they* were all crazy, so you would become impossible. That is why it is better not to go into detail about such practices in a book like this. A mention that they exist is enough, just for your information.

Cosmological science is a subject the Buddha explained with beautiful clarity. He taught that the entire universe is a reflection of every sentient being's personal karma, and that is what makes this universe their physical home. Mind has the home that is body; body has the home that is the universe. The universe has a home that is space. That is how it is described in the Tantra.

There are five elements that compose the relative material of all existence—space, which provides the foundation, then fire, water, earth, and air. These elements form every single unit of existence. Tantric science states that each of these five elements working together forms the universe. They can form galaxies and also destroy them. They can destroy the universe itself. The five elements have the power of creation and destruction.

These elements, in combination, form countless universes in endless space. A "third thousand" describes a group of 1,000 million solar systems. Since it is taught that space is filled with countless "third thousand" groups of universes, one of them is but a small spot in space. There is no end to it. Although you cannot find the end of space, the Buddha tells us you can find the middle.

Wherever you are, that is the middle of all universes. This current life may involve birth here on earth as a human being; the next life might be astronomically far from here in every way. The middle is always "here," where one takes birth.

Lord Buddha, in cosmological science, taught about how this universe and even this planet earth will develop and be destroyed. He said that this planet will be destroyed by the sun. The sun's heat will increase seven times more than what it is now, and the earth will be destroyed. Buddha said that when it is twice its present heat, most of the living beings will not exist. Most of the plants will not exist, and most of the rivers will dry up. He said that when the sun's heat is three times more, there will be no more water. There will be no more living beings with our type of physical body who need water. Humankind and animals as we know them will not exist. After a while, he said, the planet will become molten, and at the end it will become one with the sun. That is what the Buddha taught, what is in the texts. It will take a long time, though. It will not happen suddenly, so we don't have to worry about it now. The Buddha even gave a clear calculation of how many millions of centuries it will take for the sun to become hotter and for the process of destruction gradually to take place, during which time our type of life will decrease and finally disappear.

HEALING SCIENCE

Healing science is a special branch of Tantric science that utilizes the physical science of living things as well as the physical science of the universe. It is a Buddhist principle that the existence of a disease is the evidence that there is a cure. A disease cannot exist without a cure, because nothing in our relative, dualistic reality can exist without the other side. The medicine tantras are said to have been taught by Lord Buddha manifesting as the Medicine Buddha. In these he delineated all knowledge about health and healing. These medicine tantras are the basis for the practice of Tibetan medicine. It is Buddhist medicine, according to Buddhist scientific principles.

The principle of medicine is simple. It is based on the idea that the body is in harmony with this planet and the conditions of this planet. It can survive only in conditions like those on this planet. If it is put in vastly different environments, like outer space or the moon, the body cannot survive without something to protect it from whatever is lacking or excessive. The cures for bodily illness are taken from the body's own natural environment on this planet. Medicine can be found in roots, leaves, trunks of trees, flowers, fruits, and minerals, and also in parts of living things. There is medicine in all of them, antidotes for any poisons that endanger the health of the body.

Buddhist medical treatment uses such medicines as well as other methods utilizing fire, water, air, earth, and gravity. Gravity is a property of the body of earth itself. An example is the treatment for blood poisoning. A medicine concentrates the bad blood in one particular part of the body, in one particular blood vessel. That vessel is opened, and gravity used to take out the bad blood. It is a treatment in harmony with elemental principles of the universe.

Buddhist medicine also uses mathematics and astrology, because some medicines should be given only at the right time by the right person. It is a means for determining the best method of giving treatment for each individual.

The diagnostic methods most commonly used are checking the pulses and the urine. Analysis can be so fine that the health of relatives of the individual may be checked through the pulses. It is a very advanced technique. Very few people can do that—it is a special gift—and these kinds of diagnoses are called the seven amazing diagnoses. Checking the health of children through the parents is one of them. Although these things have been made very clear in the Buddhist texts, it takes years of study, application, and understanding to be an effective doctor.

MATHEMATICS

The teachings on mathematical science in the Tantras were given by Lord Manjushri, the Bodhisattva of Wisdom, who taught them on five mountains that are now located in China. Mathematics and astrology are practiced together in Vajrayana and are advanced subjects. There are roughly two areas of study, plain mathematics and mathematical calculation of the universal energy.

Plain mathematics includes the skills of calculation, some of which are extremely complex. Lord Manjushri said that mathematics can go on infinitely, but the teaching of straight calculation deals with numbers from zero to nine, and goes up to sixty digits.

Mathematics is concerned with calculating the paths of stars, planets, and the shadows of planets. Tibetan calendars are made using this kind of calculation. It is said in the texts about making a calendar that if a compete calendar is made for one day, the work will never be finished. There is so much that is possible to calculate, even if only a few figures are used. Each number in the boxes on a Tibetan calendar represents the particular angles of the universal movement, and a great deal of figuring goes into it. Yearly cycles, twelve-year cycles, and sixty-year cycles are involved, along with the elements, and a zodiac. There are, in addition, animal signs for parts of the days, the months, and so forth that correspond to the elements.

In calculating comprehensive astrological charts for individuals, even the times of birth of the parents and grandparents are taken into account. The moment of birth determines the person's entire activity. It is not that the external influences determine it, however. A person is born at a particular moment, surrounded by particular influences, because of his or her karmic causes and conditions. It is the field in which they must work in that lifetime. Astrology can often help people to understand events in their lives and learn the best ways to cope with their shortcomings and problems.

Astrology is most commonly applied to situations like building a temple, for indications about when to dig the first bit of earth, what kind of person should do it, how the temple should be situated, and so forth. It is also used to determine the best days for enterprises—for instance, when to start a retreat so that it will be the most beneficial and effective. Astrology can also determine what room the retreat should be done in, and which direction is the right one to face. Astrology and mathematics can accurately determine the interactions of universal phenomena at every moment. These sciences help with outward arrangements that support inner activities. If you rely on astrology beyond that point, however, it can become a neurotic obsession whereby you become afraid of doing anything. There is a limitation to all these sciences, and a balanced view to take of each one.

MENTAL SCIENCE

Mental science is the chief subject of Buddhism. The Vinaya, Sutras, and Tantras are devoted to mental science in many forms. Mental science concerns knowing about the mind, managing the mind, and improving the mental condition to reach the ultimate potential of the mind. Application of mental science begins in whatever situation life offers us. Life with all its conditions provides the fertile ground, because these causes and conditions in a life are unique to the same mind that has inhabited many different bodies. It is a developing mind, and the present life represents its level of development. What is happening to each of us right now has everything to do with all the past lives we have had as human beings, birds, cats, dogs, fish, or frogs, or in other realms besides the human and animal realms. We have had millions of past lives, the result of which is here, in ourselves, right now. All the causes and conditions for everything that happens to us is from that same mind and its accumulated karma. This karma ripens in different bodies, not necessarily in the same body or realm. We can be sure that wherever we will be born, our individual karma is there, like a body and its shadow.

The core of these mental causes, conditions, and results is duality. Likes and dislikes develop from duality and turn into attachment and aggression, desire and anger. That naturally gives rise to jealousy and pride, hope and fear. The Buddha, especially in Abhidharma, elaborated on all thought patterns and facets of the mind. He described fifty-one major thought patterns, which combine to form many more. He also gave methods of correcting imbalances and negativity. One of these methods, discussed earlier, is meditation.

Until enlightenment happens, everything is a process that leads toward it. Mental processes influence the physical situation. It is very clear that discomfort and comfort, attachment and anger, likes and dislikes are in the mind. Something you like very much today you may be tired of by tomorrow. You may even hate it. Nothing about it changed, only your attitude toward it. Someone else may also like what you dislike. These are psychological patterns that influence reality. They are all part of the process. This process leads to enlightenment by liberating more and more of the inherent enlightened nature. This is the purpose and end result of all Tantric science.

— *SIX* —

TRANSFORMATION

ALL BUDDHIST PRACTICES ARE METHODS OF transformation. When applied correctly, these can transform an ignorant person into a possessor of wisdom. The word *transformation*, as it is used here, signifies a change within an individual being that is a revolutionary change, but one that does not change that being's essential nature. It brings out the essential nature. Buddhist practice is a process of transformation through purification that brings out the best of what is already there. It does not make people into what they are not, nor import any new material. It allows your ultimate identity as an enlightened being to emerge as you overcome the relative delusions and defilements that mask your buddha nature. It is transformation into your ultimate self.

Buddhist practice does not change a bad person into a good one. It transforms a bad person into a better one who reflects, more and more accurately, his or her actual nature. As we have seen, this is possible because of inherent buddha nature. Ultimately there are no bad people. Ultimately everyone is good, wise, and perfect. Sometimes we can see this, even in our enemies. No matter how bad they might appear, or what terrible things they may have done, there is often something likeable or winning about our enemies. It is a spark of their inherent buddha nature showing through their negativity. Transformation from relative delusion to ultimate perfection is necessary for everyone, our enemies and ourselves. It can be done through Buddhist practice.

The pure transformed, the way it is, itself

The alchemists in the Middle Ages talked about transforming lead into gold. Lead is a worthless substance compared to gold. Alchemists looked for the special ingredient, or Philosopher's Stone, that could achieve the transformation of a more or less dull and valueless substance into a priceless one. To use the medieval alchemists' obsession to illustrate the Buddhist view of transformation, the relative world might be likened to lead, the ultimate nature to gold, and the magic ingredient to change one into the other is the true and abiding realization of buddha nature. It takes a lot of effort to reach it, but the moment of knowing is like a sudden miracle.

Sometimes we find ourselves confused. Sometimes we find other people lost in confusion. We see other people and ourselves with tremendous defilements. We usually see other people's defilements first, of course. Using the teachings of the Buddha as a guide, we eventually find that there is no one who is ultimately confused or deluded. Confusion and delusion are relative problems. With this simple understanding of the principle of transformation, we have the tool to manifest our potential. This understanding makes Dharma practice easier. We know where we are going. The goal is to realize our ultimate potential. Meditation and other methods given by the Buddha suddenly make more sense. Sitting on a cushion and calming the mind, letting insight flow in, becomes a practical, not an exotic, occupation. It is an ordinary thing, working with what we have, day after day, to achieve enlightenment.

When we try to understand someone like the Buddha, or the enlightened bodhisattvas, this idea of transformation helps us, because Buddha is precisely that, totally transformed. His ultimate potential is fully developed; there is nothing left to develop. He is free and limitless. He shows us the ultimate destiny of all sentient beings. The Buddha was once just as we are. Through his own effort, he was transformed. A bodhisattva is not yet completely transformed but close to it. A bodhisattva's potential is not yet fully developed or limitless. There is nothing ultimately different between ourselves and the Buddha but our development: relatively we are ignorant and deluded, and quite ordinary—the opposite of a totally enlightened being. But ultimately there is no difference; all the potential is there.

Understanding the transformation of relative situations into the manifestation of ultimate potential is a great step. This understanding alone can transform, in a way, a person's mundane actions. Everything we do can become a transformative act. This is the Buddha's essential advice on how to be liberated: liberation is not something you have to create, liberation is inside you. Transformation resembles the change that a moth or a butterfly must undergo. The beautiful creature that emerges from the cocoon begins life as an ugly, hairy caterpillar. After a process full of risk and pain, the adult butterfly pokes its way out of the cocoon and flies away free, on flashing, rainbow-colored wings. The butterfly was always there inside that wooly worm. Buddha nature and ultimate liberation are inside all sentient beings. After an arduous process, miraculous enlightenment comes. Sentient beings are transformed from limited, ignorant, suffering, and sometimes very bad individuals into limitless, wise, and compassionate bodhisattvas who eventually become enlightened buddhas. The Buddha taught the method of transformation in meticulous detail. Buddhism shows the way to transform every defilement into wisdom, every limitation into limitless freedom. That is Buddhism when seen from the perspective of transformation.

MEANS OF TRANSFORMATION

Conventional Buddhist practice begins by taking refuge in the Buddha, the Dharma, and the Sangha. A person formally becomes a Buddhist by doing this. It might be said that every sentient being is a natural Buddhist, because all beings have buddha nature. So taking refuge is just a formality.

This understanding of Buddhism—as a living essence within each being—transcends the limitation of Buddhism perceived as a particular denomination or religion. Buddhism is, in fact, limited by its name. It has become an "ism," and it has been put into a convenient and superficial pigeonhole. Buddhism is turned into an excuse to form societies and make it into a business. None of this has much to do with the actual teachings. There is a reason for this sort of thing happening, of course. That is the way human beings always relate to things; it is part of the delusion. It cannot be avoided. With this in mind, people should look beyond the trappings into actual Buddhist practice. Real Buddhist practice does not require expensive Japanese gongs or bells, Tibetan carpets and carved tables, Chinese porcelain offering bowls, or a Ming dynasty Buddha statue. It takes honest self-assessment, contemplation, and a moment-to-moment commitment to shed the cocoon of delusion. This can be done in any language, any kind of outfit, in rooms with any kind of decor.

Taking refuge in the Buddha, the Dharma, and the Sangha is the beginning. One takes refuge in the Buddha as the example. The Buddha is the ultimately realized teacher. The Buddha is also the aim. One takes refuge in the Dharma teachings as the path, a way to achieve the aim, through gradual progress. The Sangha are the teachers who are guides on the path, and friends who offer help in learning. The Buddhist "taking refuge" is not the ordinary sense of refuge, where you depend on somebody or something that could collapse at any time. The Buddha, Dharma, and Sangha are sources of spiritual refuge that are reliable always.

Refuge taken properly is a transformational act. It is, conventionally, the first step to transformation. But that is a superficial view of it. A being may have taken that transformational step a long time ago, maybe many lifetimes ago. Taking refuge in this life is a formal way to affirm or reaffirm the commitment to transformation.

Taking refuge in the Buddha gives an aspirant to enlightenment a limitless source of confidence and inspiration. There is nothing about the Buddha that cannot be trusted. Correct refuge should be like that: a person is able to have complete and unshakable trust in something, in the Buddha. That is possible, and not dangerous, because the Buddha is a fully enlightened being who will not lead anyone astray. Profound faith may be established right there, at the beginning. There is a transformation at that moment in the person who takes refuge. From having no trust in anything after a lifetime of being disappointed by unreliable, ordinary objects of refuge, one is able to gain a limitless, secure, and well-founded confidence in an enlightened, transcendent being who has succeeded in the most impressive accomplishment of all.

Another level of taking refuge in the Buddha is seeing buddhahood as the aim or purpose of existence. We continue to improve until we become buddha, which is our highest possible achievement. A buddha develops from a very ordinary, deluded reality, the same place every person taking refuge starts out. The buddha then attains limitless realization. Knowing this, a person taking refuge acquires a purpose, knows the ultimate potential, and knows the goal. It is undeniably beneficial to change from a weak person victimized by delusion, without purpose or confidence, to one who is secure in knowledge of purpose.

Taking refuge in the Dharma takes this evolution of confidence a step further by providing the means to achieve the goal. Without a method, the idea of enlightenment is nothing more than a theoretical possibility. The Dharma is the teaching that defines the step-by-step process we must go through to move out of our present state of ignorance into greater and greater insight and realization. The people who heard the historical Buddha teach had limitations. Time was a limitation. The Buddha could not transmit more than 84,000 different methods in his years of teaching. Yet these methods will work for all the different beings with their various limitations and needs. There are enough methods for us all to achieve enlightenment. We can have complete confidence in a path that gets us to our destination if followed according to the clear directions that have been given. A person who keeps getting stuck in confusion and pain due to ignorance about how to improve is transformed by the very knowledge that there are specific instructions, a clearly marked map, of how to move ahead and be gradually liberated, until guided to final enlightenment.

The Sangha are individuals—bodhisattvas, spiritual teachers, and spiritual friends—with whose help we can progress. These are people from whom we learn, with whom we practice, with whom we share experiences along the spiritual path. That is the Sangha in the Tibetan Buddhist meaning of the word. The teaching of Buddha is profound, and if there were no Sangha, it would be very difficult for ordinary people to understand. One might find a wonderful subject, look through volumes about it, and try to understand and do the practice, but something will be missing. How can you be sure you understand it or are doing it right? Without the guidance of someone who has had the specific mind transmission and done the practices, you cannot be sure you are doing it right. How can someone know that of which they have no experience? Without correct instruction and guided experience, you can only make more errors, sometimes serious ones that will delay your progress.

The Sangha are the followers of the Buddha who are already practicing the teachings, who have carried the instruction given by the Buddha to the present, after 2,500 years of unbroken lineage transmission. We learn from the Sangha and know that the instruction is correct, pure, and undeviated. It has been tested by masters and passed on, to be tested again and again. This transmission comes with a powerful blessing that has been strengthened by devotion and compassion. It was given at the time of the Buddha to his disciples, who passed it on from that time to other dedicated disciples, who became practitioners and teachers. A lot of energy has accumulated in the teachings over centuries of transmission.

Taking refuge in the Sangha is the first step toward receiving this same transmission and benefiting from the experiences of all those who have received it before you. There is the blessing, the profound guidance, and the profound instruction. By taking refuge in the Sangha, you find the right company, people in whom you can have confidence, right guidance that you can count on, and the blessing from the Buddha, up to now unbroken. So it is similar to taking refuge in Dharma. Dharma is the teaching. Taking refuge goes hand in hand with taking refuge in the Dharma, because the Sangha transmits the teaching. It is important, of course, to consider the teacher carefully, to make sure he or she has the qualifications, which not only depend on knowledge but on experience, a degree of realization, and compassionate behavior. For this there are guidelines also.

The next level of activity leading to transformation is bodhichitta, very important in both the Mahayana and Vajrayana Buddhist traditions. Bodhichitta and the four ways to engender it—loving-kindness, compassion, joy, impartiality—are essential for transformation. Without this, progress cannot be made because one remains stuck in petty jealousies, attachment, resentment, pride, and ignorance. People without bodhichitta suffer when they see the success of others and suffer more intensely from their own misfortunes. Bodhichitta turns this around and makes everyone's happiness a source of joy. Even your own misfortunes become a cause for happiness, because they are opportunities to learn from and purify negative karma. This is a kind of transformation that alters our lives in samsara tremendously. Life becomes not only bearable, but a joyful source of further progress. Developing bodhichitta does this. Although there is a ceremony to mark the commitment to bodhichitta—taking the Bodhisattva Vow—the real thing is inside, the actual generation of bodhichitta day in and day out. It is a significant transformation that is continuous, as long as bodhichitta is there.

MEDITATION METHODS: CALMING THE MIND AND INSIGHT

Meditation practices are an important means of development, and the two basic methods are *shamatha* and *vipassana* meditation, in English, "calming the mind" and "insight meditation." In Tibetan these are called *shinay* and *lhatong*. The purpose of *shinay* is to develop calmness, and the purpose of *lhatong* is to develop clarity. Calmness and clarity are related, and they come together, but the explanation and the practice divides them into two steps.

The necessity of *shinay* comes from the overwhelming influence of samsara on sentient beings. Samsara, as we have seen, is the endless manifestation of illusion based on ignorance and perpetuated by the twelve interdependent links. In the face of unmitigated samsaric influence, the real potential of an individual sentient being becomes lost, because behavior is governed by delusion. A human being, for example, can become obsessed by desire, anger, jealousy, or pride, and falls into profound ignorance when obsessed by any one of them. Samsara is full of the causes and conditions for these obsessions. To free oneself from those influences, a certain kind of strength must be developed. Such strength of mind comes from meditation practices like *shinay*.

Shinay transforms a person easily influenced by the physical, mental, and emotional factors in the environment into a person who can be steady and calm despite outer influences. It transforms a person who is insecure because everything affects him or her into a person who can take charge, who feels secure because he or she can see what is going on in his or her life so much more clearly due to a calm mind. Most of us are bothered by doubts about ourselves, because we find we cannot trust even ourselves. We cover up these inadequacies because we cannot bear to see our own confusion and accept that we are insecure and ignorant. We spend our energy covering up, and we do not progress. Despite all our pretending, we still cannot avoid reality. We eventually get ourselves into trouble. By not seeing things as they are, we make a small thing into a huge problem. It is like one small spark of fire that hits the dry grass in the mountains and burns hundreds of acres of forested land. The practice of *shinay* meditation helps a person see what the real problem is and handle it in the most energy-efficient way. Weakness, strength, and shortcomings are seen in the clear mirror of a calm mind. When the mind is at rest, it is easy to see things clearly. *Shinay* meditation makes your mind calm. This calmness of mind transforms the individual. A life complicated because the individual is at the mercy of outside influences becomes blissfully simple. Problems seen clearly and honestly can be solved without wasting precious time or energy. People who are able to do this are capable, secure, knowledgeable, even wise people. They can look at things calmly. *Shinay* meditation can bring this gift into our lives.

Lhatong is the clear quality, the profound potential, that is developed through the peace and calm of *shinay*. It is said that without *shinay* and *lhatong* development, it is difficult to do anything positive. Negative actions come very easily to ordinary people; for them, it is often easier to do negative things than positive things. Once *shinay* and *lhatong* are developed, the ability to perform positive actions becomes equal to the ability to perform negative ones. The greater the development, the easier it becomes to do positive things and the more difficult it is to do negative things. That is the sort of transformation of attitude and habit that comes about through calming the mind and the clarity of *lhatong,* or insight meditation.

FIVE DEFILEMENTS AND THE FIVE WISDOMS

The teaching of the five defilements that transform into five wisdoms, each of which is represented by a Buddha family, comes from the Tantric teachings. Tantra is one of the four categories of teachings given by Lord Buddha. These categories were not made by Buddha himself but evolved when his disciples compiled the teachings into Vinaya, Sutra, Abhidharma, and Tantra. Although the teaching on the five defilements and five wisdoms is mentioned in some of the sutras, it is precisely taught and practices are given in the Tantras.

Ignorance is the absence of wisdom. When you do not have wisdom, you have ignorance. Ignorance and wisdom are connected. They are like the two sides of the hand. That is how the defilements are taught in Tantra. Because we do not realize that our ultimate potential is wisdom, we remain in ignorance. Through our ignorance, however, we can ultimately gain wisdom.

Tantra is advanced teaching, and it is not possible to limit the relationship between the five defilements and five wisdoms to one fixed pattern. Within Tantra, the teachings and practices evolve. That is the quality of Tantra, which addresses the many facets of reality. There is really no hard and fast formula for the interaction of the five defilements and five wisdoms, although a general, basic description may be given. The defilements are, of course, the negative patterns of thought and action, and the different aspects of wisdom are the positive patterns of thought and action. The connection between the two involves two sides of the ultimate potential.

So the essence of ignorance has another side, the wisdom of Dharma space. It is like the essence of emptiness, where there is space for everything. This is represented by the Buddha Vairochana.

Ego or pride is transformed into the wisdom of equanimity, which is represented by Ratnasambhava. Desire or attachment is transformed into discriminating wisdom and is associated with the Buddha Amitabha. Jealousy is transformed into all-accomplishing wisdom, represented by the Buddha Amogasiddhi. Anger or aggression is linked to mirrorlike wisdom, in which everything shines. It is emptiness that is like a mirror, and all existence can be reflected from it because of the emptiness. It is similar to saying that everything can happen relatively because ultimately nothing is happening. This is associated with the Buddha Ashokbya.

This is how transformation is understood from the Tantric point of view: every negative thing is seen as ultimately positive. Therefore, if you transform the negativity, it naturally becomes positive, because that is its ultimate essence. Everything is related in the Tantric point of view. The reason for ignorance is its ultimate potential, wisdom. Transformation as a Tantric principle is very important, and a person who can practice correctly is able to transform all the defilements into wisdom. Merely wanting to practice the Tantric method to transform defilements is not sufficient, though. The foundation must be built first so the individual becomes capable of and ready for advanced methods by doing the appropriate preliminary practices leading up to that stage. Only then can the transformation take place. Then it works; otherwise it will not.

Buddha said that a qualified Tantric practitioner can attain enlightenment quite quickly when he or she understands that the principle of transformation is active in all aspects of life and practice. If a person has many defilements but sincerely tries to practice Tantric method and puts forth every effort, the Buddha said it will take about sixteen lifetimes to attain complete enlightenment. This is with sincere and dedicated practice, something that is very rarely seen. The Buddha also said that with the Tantric method, enlightenment can be attained in one second. Why? Of course, because we are buddhas, ultimately. If you fully realize that, then buddhahood manifests in you. The Buddha is not talking about a glimpse during meditation, but total, profound realization. And although enlightenment will not even take a split second, we must remember always that the ability to have that realization arises from years and lifetimes of effort. So the Buddha's words do not mean we can be lazy. We cannot relax just because the Tantric method is there and expect to become buddha automatically. We must work hard at it.

We are fortunate if we recognize our potential and became a Buddhist because of that recognition, because we have chosen a very effective path. We are also very fortunate that the Buddha's teaching is alive now. This teaching is not just a set of texts in the library. It is alive. It lives in the teachings passed down directly from the Buddha, through generations of teachers; it lives in advice and commentaries written down by enlightened masters.

There is one very important text written by a great master called Phadampa Sangye, one of many that he wrote. In it he says about practice, "You can test yourself. If the antidote comes as soon as the defilement comes, then you are practicing well. If the antidote is not there when you need it, and defilements take over, then you are not doing well. You have to practice more." It is a piece of valuable advice.

He says, "Devotion without compassion is not complete.

Compassion without devotion is not complete. You have to have compassion and devotion together for completion." He goes on to say, "Happiness and fortunate situations do not always have good results, so do not be proud of your good fortune and happiness, and do not indulge in it too much. Suffering is not always bad. There are many things to be learned from negative situations and suffering. Therefore you should not be discouraged when misfortunes come." He also advised that practitioners should not wait for conditions they do not have. You should use whatever conditions you have now. That is very important.

"Sectarianism, liking and disliking the teachings, is one of the biggest obstacles and most shameful things that can arise in a Dharma practitioner, and should be avoided," Phadampa Sangye advised. He said, "There are no end to thoughts and imagination. Think only those things that are worth thinking. Do not spend your time on meaningless thoughts."

One last helpful observation of his is, "Ego is the most evilly powerful thing, so always watch out for your ego."

When the Buddha taught, he was not limited in what he could teach, but people who listen hear what they are able to hear. Some people's potential is good, so enlightenment is fast. Some people's potential is not liberated to a high degree, so it takes a long time. Some people have more defilements, some people have fewer defilements, so the path to enlightenment may take a longer or shorter time, depending on the individual. Different methods work for different people; one method may speed a person to enlightenment, and another may go at a slower pace, according to individual need. A method suitable for one person may not be suitable for another. The only way to enlightenment is to go at your own pace of transformation.

Our guidance comes from a teacher with profound understanding and experience. We should not compare ourselves to others or try to reach for the moon and feel disappointed when we fail. As Phadampa Sangye says, work with the conditions that your life presents. Even the most humdrum day is full of potential moments of transformation. Look at the teaching of the Buddha realistically, not from a narrow or inflated point of view. All human beings are not the same height, weight, or coloring. They do not look the same. Everybody is slightly different. We all achieve enlightenment through a unique process of transformation.

——— *SEVEN* ———

ENLIGHTENMENT

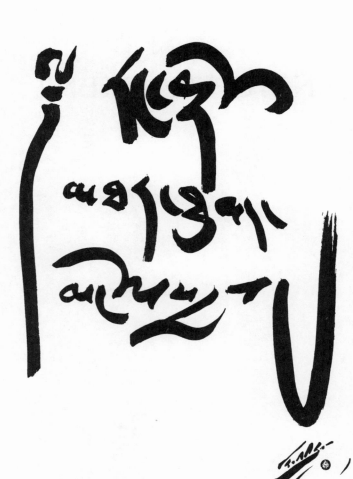

ALTHOUGH IT IS IMPOSSIBLE TO KNOW WHAT enlightenment is until we are enlightened ourselves, it is important to gain as much intellectual understanding as possible about it. All levels of Buddhist teaching stress that every sentient being is perfect in the ultimate sense. It is this perfect potential that is not yet awakened and developed that gives us our great destiny of buddhahood, or enlightenment. A sentient being who is not enlightened is a sentient being in samsara, the self-perpetuating delusion, or what may be called the relative world. Those sentient beings who are enlightened are known as buddhas.

The word *buddha* itself, *sang gye* in Tibetan, describes this state quite clearly. *Sang* means awakened. *Gye* means developed. So *sang gye* means fully awakened and fully developed, a term that explicitly describes the state of complete enlightenment. To reach that final moment of enlightenment, it might take billions of lifetimes directed toward that end. When that moment arrives, when all the effort bears fruit and the individual has fully developed awakening, then the ultimate destination, buddhahood, is reached.

With this simple definition as a basis, it is possible to examine the different levels of realization, some of which we have already considered, such as the *bhumi*s, the levels of bodhisattva realization. There are many levels of realization before final enlightenment. It is not possible to go into each step because it is a moment-to-moment process. The instant you aspire to be better, a degree of realization takes place. The idea and understanding

---

Liberation is ultimate enlightenment

that you can be better and want to be better is itself a realization. Following from this moment, until the moment you become better, to the moment you gain a deeper understanding and have a deeper aspiration to improve, every moment becomes a moment of realization. It is impossible to go through it all in a book, but one will experience these insights as one progresses gradually.

There are a few particular levels of realization that are taught in Buddhism, and discussing them may clarify a little the process toward enlightenment. When a person becomes aware that he or she should improve, in whatever area, it is then that a person naturally begins seeking effective methods to liberate innate potential. Enlightenment starts from there. One of the major accomplishments, as given in the texts, is called "one-pointed human mind." This is the highest level of development that is possible within the physical, emotional, and mental limitations of the human realm. One can develop the one-pointed, clear mind in this human environment using some of the techniques we have already discussed. Development of clarity makes beneficial actions natural. When this happens, negative actions take a tremendous effort to perform, and positive actions come spontaneously. One is able to see things correctly without trying. That is how far we can get with this human body, its expression, and its relationship to the mind. It is the highest level of achievement possible for an ordinary being, utilizing only what is offered in this human realm. Beyond this, extraordinary practices are necessary for development. More advanced individuals may inhabit human bodies, but their accomplishments are drawn from other, higher levels of mind.

This highest human level of realization may be achieved through basic meditation techniques and regulation of our lives through moral, physical, and mental discipline. It is achieved by using the limited human realm with its emotions, physical characteristics, and environment. When these factors are utilized in a correct and balanced way, the result is what might be called a perfect human being, an unconditionally good and wise person within the bounds of the human realm. One-pointed human mind—that is, becoming a perfect human being—is our first goal. We must personify the best potential of a human being, with all the human feelings and desires: a human being who intentionally strives to get the best out of the worst situations; a human being who faces reality without having to make excuses, ignore certain things, or pretend; a human being who is able to handle what is going on in life, as it is. A perfect human being can function in whatever situation comes up, handle it, and not be adversely affected by it. Rather, everything is used for benefit. This is the foundation for enlightenment, which continues, in stages, from one-pointed human mind.

The next level of realization goes beyond the limitation of human emotions, environment, and physical existence. That is the level of *mahasiddhas*, or accomplished practitioners. The level of realization of a *mahasiddha* and of a great bodhisattva, or Compassionate One, is beyond the limited human environment and physical influence. *Mahasiddhas* and enlightened bodhisattvas recognize the relativity of external existence, the inner emotions, and the play of thoughts. Because of their recognition and profound understanding of relative reality, they have less limitation than the perfect human being on the level of one-pointed mind.

One difference between the human and the higher levels of attainment is that the perfect, kind, and wise person can manifest in only one incarnation, or emanation, at a time. The *mahasiddhas* and enlightened bodhisattvas can manifest in multiple forms at the same time. When a *mahasiddha* or bodhisattva realizes the relativity of time, external existence, emotions, and other phenomena, the influence of external realities becomes irrelevant as a form of limitation. The human body's influence on the emotions is irrelevant. Rather, such individuals become masters of the phenomena of the human realm; the relative realities become tools for them. That is how miracles are performed by great bodhisattvas and enlightened *mahasiddhas*. They have transcended the boundaries through their profound understanding. That is why they are able to walk through walls.

Such an ability is not a superficial magical technique, it is a genuine miracle, and it arises from a different source. It comes from the individual's realization of the relative and ultimate nature of reality and the essential emptiness of everything. The spiritual master who can perform miracles, because of his or her profound understanding, is not affected by the dualistic influence of external relative reality. *Mahasiddhas* and bodhisattvas are free of duality within themselves; therefore, their extraordinary relationship with the external reality of ordinary people becomes a miraculous event. The great *mahasiddhas* who perform miracles such as going beyond time and going beyond the influence of an element—for example, walking on water, rising up in the air, sitting on a blade of grass, or influencing the elements, as in making or stopping rain—demonstrate their mastery and realization of the relativity of external existence. Time, space, and matter may be manipulated by them at the subtlest level. The emanation of a first-level bodhisattva at 100 locations at once is a miracle in our ordinary experience, unbelievable for many ordinary people, but it is normal for the bodhisattvas. Those who can perform miracles, it is important to point out, are motivated by compassion, loving-kindness, and wisdom, and they do so for the purpose of benefiting others.

It is not quite the right motivation to want to become a bodhisattva and a practitioner of Buddhism because you want miraculous power. The motivation should be to achieve enlightenment to be able to help all sentient beings. The miraculous power is a by-product, something that happens in the process of enlightenment, but it is not a goal in itself. It is very wrong as well as a waste of time to practice Buddhism because you want magical powers. If people want to start learning magic, there is a simple way to start: join a magicians' association. Then you will learn something, and you won't have to practice Buddhism to do it. It's a totally different thing.

When the great bodhisattva attains enlightenment, buddhahood, that is the final step of realization. There is nothing more to realize. There is nothing more to develop. To try to explain this enlightenment is a challenging undertaking, but thanks to the Buddha himself and the great masters of the past, we can learn about it. They made an impossible task possible. There are two angles of approach. One is to define enlightenment itself, and the other is to examine how it manifests—what it is and how it appears.

Right now, enlightenment is within us as the ultimate essence of our minds. Although it pervades us as the ultimate essence of our minds, we still do not quite understand it. We have many questions and doubts. We may even doubt we have a mind at all. Many people doubt that, and they might spend hundreds of lifetimes finding out about it. The questions and doubts may go on for lifetimes, but our ultimate, essentially purified nature is always present.

This essence, through discipline and effort, is gradually unveiled, and its qualities are liberated. The liberation can continue over a long time, until the final manifestation and liberation of buddhahood. Then the limitless qualities that have so long been only potential are completely freed. That is enlightenment.

It is possible to have an experience of the pure, limitless quality of mind when we sit and meditate. It is merely a glimpse, but we can have a taste of it if our meditation is good. When meditation is right, it is one of the experiences that may come. We can also glimpse it in extreme situations, such as when we are exhilarated about something wonderful in our lives or if we have a near-death experience. If we were to look at our minds at such times, we would see that, actually, nothing is happening to the mind. But if we look at our emotions, a great deal is going on there. This is true whether the experience produces happiness or suffering. As far as the nature of our mind is concerned, nothing is happening. The glimpse of enlightenment is a moment when we are able to see everything just as it is.

There is a saying about ignorance and wisdom: Nothing can create more damage than ignorance, and nothing can benefit more than wisdom. Wisdom sees and understands, whereas ignorance is not knowing, not understanding. Even if the world explodes, it can only destroy this body, not this mind. It cannot delay realization, not even for a second. Ignorance, on the other hand, can delay realization for millions of lifetimes. The whole universe is on our side, in a sense, trying to bring us to realization. If you do not have wisdom and do not understand, no one can make you understand or realize anything. When you have wisdom, then you realize. When you develop wisdom, enlightenment can follow. So there is a great benefit in developing wisdom, and tremendous harm in ignorance and pride.

The limitless potential of the mind, when it is fully liberated, makes activity, understanding, wisdom, compassion—everything—limitless. You are buddha, beyond any limitation. A buddha is free from the burdens of time, matter, causes, and conditions. If all the sentient beings in existence wholeheartedly pray to the Buddha at the same time, the Buddha's blessing in response can reach them all equally and at the same time. Each being may perceive the blessing differently, though, according to his or her karma. They may all receive a different teaching at that moment. In Tantric terms, this aspect of a buddha who manifests and teaches limitlessly is called the *dharmakaya*. This is the vehicle of enlightenment, the *dharmakaya*.

The next consideration is how enlightenment appears, how it manifests. This depends on each individual in whom it manifests. There are, generally speaking, two major classifications. The first and higher category is made up of those who are highly enlightened, above first-level bodhisattva realization. The second, lower, category consists of those who are not enlightened, the ordinary sentient beings. That includes the kind, wise, and perfected human beings. The traditional explanation of how enlightenment appears is through describing the three *kayas*, or forms, because it is through these forms that enlightenment manifests to the various levels of beings.

The three *kayas* are *dharmakaya, sambhogakaya,* and *nirmanakaya.* The term *Dharma* signifies everything, all phenomena, existence as well as emptiness. *Dharmakaya* is the form that is the essence of everything, the embodiment of everything. *Sambhoga* means complete, nothing left out, nothing excluded. *Sambhogakaya* is the body of total development. *Nirmanakaya* means emanation or manifestation of mind in a physical body. An individual, depending on his or her development, can manifest in one or countless forms at the same time. When a person becomes enlightened, the mind is *dharmakaya;* the energy, speech, and expression are *sambhogakaya;* and the physical body is *nirmanakaya.*

The mind that we are aware of now learns, thinks, understands, gets confused, and so forth because it is clouded by defilements. Which is more limited, the body or the mind? The body is definitely more limited. The mind, wherever it may be right now, can expand to infinite awareness. It is essentially limitless in potential, although its present state, relatively, may be small due to the basic misunderstanding called samsara. We constantly limit the limitless potential of the mind by putting it into a small box called "I." That is how mind, which is limitless, becomes limited. In one of the sacred prayers of the Mahamudra

lineage, the Mahamudra Prayer by the third Karmapa, it is mentioned very clearly that one constantly encounters the limitless
essence of oneself, but one constantly misunderstands it as "I."
Dharmakaya embodies that ultimate limitless quality, the actual
nature of the mind, completely purified and realized.

One prayer that is often recited is to the buddhas of the ten
directions, who teach the profound teachings for the benefit of
all sentient beings. It signifies the diversity of the ways in which
the countless sentient beings may attain enlightenment, "in all
directions." It does not mean that Tibetan Buddhism is the only
way to attain enlightenment, but that the right method, the right
path can be found anywhere there is clarity and truth. When
that method is pursued, beings attain enlightenment. That is another way to view the limitless quality of the *dharmakaya*.

Mind becomes fully manifested *dharmakaya* when enlightenment is attained. Fully enlightened expression, or speech, is
manifested in *sambhogakaya*. *Dharmakaya* is only to be experienced when an individual attains the enlightenment of buddhahood, but *sambhogakaya* is experienced by others. Only highly
developed individuals are able to perceive the buddha *sambhogakaya*. *Sambhogakaya* has five characteristics that describe it.
There are detailed explanations of the three *kayas* in the texts,
but these are too involved for our purpose here. What follows is
a brief outline of these characteristics.

FIVE CHARACTERISTICS OF *SAMBHOGAKAYA*

The first characteristic is how *sambhogakaya* manifests in those
who are highly developed. The chief characteristic is that there
will be no cause or condition of wrongdoing or negativity. Nothing will make the individual experience anger, attachment, jealousy, or ego. That means the environment becomes something
like a perfect environment, in the same way that a human being
can become a perfect human being. The *sambhogakaya* is the

purified and perfect external environment that induces nothing but good to happen. This *sambhogakaya* environment is known as the Sambhogakaya Pure Land. Such Pure Lands exist wherever a buddha is manifesting.

The same thing happens with time. The texts say that time in the Sambhogakaya Pure Land is beyond limitation. Within the limitation of time, most of the past is forgotten, the future is unknown, and the present is often somehow missed. When *sambhogakaya* manifests, time becomes free of all these hindrances and distortions. Omniscience, knowing the future, knowing the past—all this becomes normal here.

The third characteristic of *sambhogakaya* manifestation is completeness. The individual has everything, all wisdom, all beneficial qualities, and becomes the complete embodiment of realization. Nothing is missing. The person manifesting *sambhogakaya* becomes a source of blessing, a source of wisdom, a source of everything that is limitless and ultimate.

The fourth characteristic has to do with who will experience the Sambhogakaya Pure Land. That level of enlightened accomplishment is experienced only by those who are highly developed, those who have advanced beyond the first *bhumi* of bodhisattva realization.

The fifth characteristic involves the expression and influence of the *sambhogakaya*. Up to this point, it has been described as perfect surroundings, perfect time perception, and perfect embodiment of enlightened qualities, and it has perfect beings to experience it. The activity generated from this perfection is the teaching of the fruition, or result. It becomes the ultimate teaching, the ultimate manifestation, that will upgrade the other beings from their level, which is already quite highly developed, to becoming even closer to buddhahood. Everything that manifests from this *sambhogakaya* causes those who experience it to become what it is, enlightened. It is the final teaching, the fruition teaching. So those are the five particulars that describe *sambho-gakaya*.

When one becomes a buddha, the mind is *dharmakaya*, the subtle body is *sambhogakaya,* and the physical body is *nirmana-kaya*. *Nirmanakaya* is experienced by all sentient beings. It is the way human beings who are not that highly developed—ordinary human beings, animals, spirits, every kind of sentient being—will perceive a buddha. *Nirmanakaya* is the emanation body or the manifestation body. There are a few particular ways the buddha manifests to ordinary sentient beings: as a friend, as an inspiration, as a teacher, or simply as a cause and condition for making that person develop, making that person become a better person. The Buddha's teaching will be the right word at the right time. The words repeated here are examples of the right word, words taught by Shakyamuni Buddha. These words are actually a part of the Buddha's *nirmanakaya,* which still continues, alive after 2,500 years.

Lord Buddha very clearly said in the teachings that right now the body is the seed of *nirmanakaya,* speech is the seed of *sambhogakaya,* and mind is the seed of *dharmakaya*. We can see the great difference between a perfect human being and what we call enlightenment after examining the characteristics of each state. There is a tremendous difference between these two. Yet, if you perfect this body, speech, and mind through perfect action and perfect intention, and with methods such as meditation, then that essence, that seed, becomes fully liberated. That is why every last sentient being has the potential for manifesting *dharmakaya, sambhogakaya,* and *nirmanakaya*. Many sutras describe the human birth as the best vehicle for enlightenment, but all sentient beings have that potential.

A very simple analogy can be given about the different levels of realization. When you learn how to read, first you have to learn about the alphabet—*a, b, c, d*—the shape of each letter, and so forth. It can be complicated for children, or even for adults when they are learning a new language. It takes time to master. Once the alphabet is mastered, you learn to put the letters together to make words: *a-p-p-l-e* makes *apple*. After that, you learn grammar and vocabulary; eventually you learn to read simple things, and later very difficult and complicated things. Like learning to read, enlightenment or realization is a gradual process. There is no such thing as sudden enlightenment. The moment of enlightenment comes after a long process of learning, development, and realization that lasts lifetimes. The Buddha may have become fully enlightened at the age of thirty-five in the lifetime when he was born Siddhartha Gautama, the son of the king of the Sakyas, but his enlightenment did not come only from the bit of practice he did in that lifetime. It was the fruition of millions of lifetimes of development.

For those who are highly enlightened, *dharmakaya* manifests in a particular way because their level of realization is closer to *dharmakaya*. The environment of *dharmakaya* will manifest to those who are highly enlightened as a Pure Land. The time of *dharmakaya* will manifest to those highly enlightened as changeless and unshakable. For those who are highly enlightened, the *dharmakaya* will be a perfect manifestation. Nothing is lacking, nothing is missing, everything is perfect and complete. In Tantric terms, this is called *sambhogakaya*.

When the *dharmakaya* manifests to ordinary sentient beings who are not highly enlightened, its manifestation is dependent on their capacity to experience it. The manifestation of *dharmakaya* will allow the ordinary sentient being to become a highly enlightened sentient being and create the circumstances for that to happen. The *dharmakaya* manifestation will facilitate ordinary sentient beings' recognition of the relativity and impermanence of time and circumstance. The manifestation of *dharmakaya* at this level will help ordinary sentient beings realize how they can purify their environment and improve. It will help the ordinary sentient beings overcome the defilements present in thoughts and emotions.

Dharmakaya manifestation is not limited, and it will always help ordinary sentient beings improve and gain higher realization. It can only be of benefit. It cannot cause ordinary sentient beings to have more delusion, but it will help them overcome delusion. The manifestation of *dharmakaya* for ordinary sentient beings is called *nirmanakaya*. These *kayas* are emanations of the buddha mind. They are not three different things.

The aim of every sentient being is to be enlightened. This abiding goal is not something that is usually outwardly recognized, but it is there inside. When we get everything right—our meditation, our actions, the pattern of our lives—this ultimate potential of ours will fully awaken. Right now within us, our mind is *dharmakaya;* our speech, or expression, is *sambhogakaya;* and our body is *nirmanakaya*. Because we are not enlightened yet, it does not appear this way. Relatively we have many problems with all these three areas of body, speech, and mind. That is samsara, the obstacles that block our clear perception of *dharmakaya, sambhogakaya,* and *nirmanakaya*. If we cannot even perceive it, we cannot manifest it. Our lack of recognition is ignorance. All the other defilements are products of that ignorance. Enlightenment is when we finally get this message in the clearest and most irrevocable way. Defilements are completely purified: we become buddha. The Buddhist wish is that we all will recognize this potential. The "we" includes sentient beings who are our friends and our enemies, those that live under a rock, that inhabit the sea, or who live far beyond the knowledge of this small planet earth—enlightenment for all sentient beings. That is the purest ambition of every Buddhist.

—— *EIGHT* ——
MAHAMUDRA

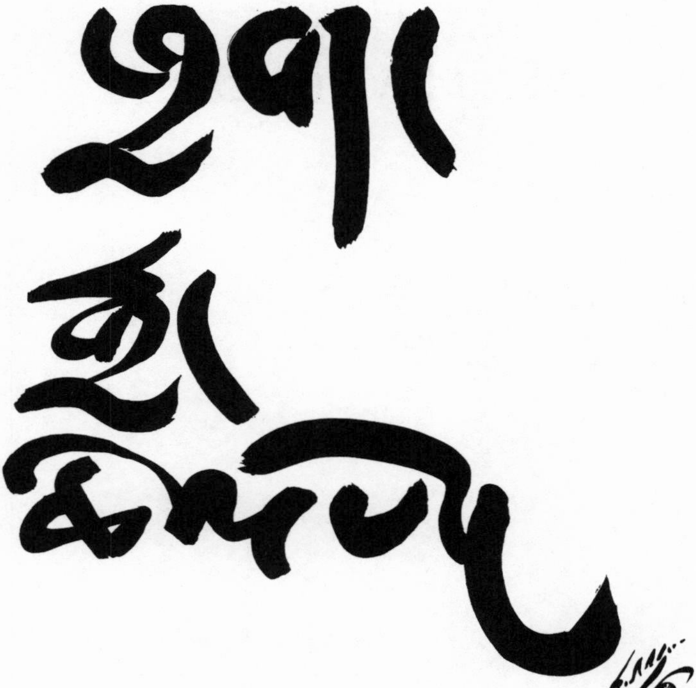

THE WORD *MAHAMUDRA* ITSELF CONTAINS THE essence of its teaching. *Mahamudra* is a Sanskrit term. Translated into Tibetan, it is *phyag rgya chen po*. The Sanskrit word *mudra* in Tibetan is *phyag rgya*, which means gesture, movement, or symbol. The Sanskrit word *maha* in Tibetan is *chen po*, meaning great or grand, and it can also convey the sense of endlessness and limitlessness. These two words together represent all phenomena, all the gestures or movements of the universe, and the limitlessness and endlessness of all manifestation, which is manifestation from one source. That is the beginning of an understanding of Mahamudra. Every manifestation of the relative world is a gesture of the ultimate essence.

The next level of understanding of Mahamudra, as explained in the commentaries, is the idea that all phenomena, physical or mental, are sealed with ultimate essence. It is like a paper signed and sealed. One can attain liberation through anything, because the essence of everything is ultimate truth. Ultimate truth is the mark all phenomena bear. Mahamudra is the name of a particular type of Buddhist teaching that embodies all teachings. It is a distillation of all the teachings in one. The Mahamudra itself is a specialized teaching.

The source of any teaching in Buddhism is the teaching of the Buddha. Any commentaries written by his disciples and later learned masters, from Buddha until the present time, are based on the Buddha's words as set down in the Sutras and Tantras. It is an unbroken lineage of transmission from the Buddha's time, the kind of transmission that is absolutely necessary to ensure correct practice and achievement when using Buddhist methods.

The particular sources of Mahamudra teaching are three: the words of the Buddha, the commentaries, and the oral instruction. In Tibetan the words of the Buddha are called *ka,* which actually means "command." The designation for those texts translated into Tibetan from the Indian language, Sanskrit, is *jajung.* These texts were brought by scholars to Tibet beginning about 1,000 years ago, and they form the basis of the Tibetan Buddhist canon, the Kangyur and the Tengyur. *Menga* means oral transmission, that is, instruction from teacher to disciple. Some of the Tantras in which the Mahamudra is specifically taught are *Guhyasamaja, Chakrasamvara, Hevajra, Mahamaya,* and *Kalachakra.* In many of the Tantras of this level, the essential teaching is Mahamudra.

One of the categories of texts translated from Sanskrit, the Tengyr, contains the commentaries written by the followers of the Buddha in India. They were the great *mahapandita*s and great enlightened ones of India during the early days of Buddhism. Indrabhuti, one of the eighty-four *mahasiddha*s, wrote a text called the *Yeshe Trupa,* or "The Accomplishment of Wisdom." It is an example of the sort of text found in the commentaries.

One of the eight greatest scholars and enlightened masters in Buddhist history is Nagarjuna. One of the texts written by Nagarjuna clearly explains the Mahamudra. This is another commentary. Another of the eight great masters, Aryadeva, wrote a text entitled *Purification of the Mind.* This also is one of the sources of Mahamudra.

Nagarjuna, Aryadeva, and Vasubhandu—along with Asanga, who received the Five Teachings of Lord Maitreya—are among the great masters of India who wrote texts concerning Mahamudra. Saraha is another master who wrote four texts that go together. One concerns the body, another the speech, the third the mind, and the last one discusses all three together.

There are a few texts that were given by the great bodhisattvas such as Lord Maitreya and Avalokiteshvara. Their teaching is also a source of Mahamudra. The teaching of the Bodhisattva Avalokiteshvara, such as *sem nyi mar tso,* or "resting the mind," and the teaching of Lord Maitreya, the *Mahayana-anuttara-tantra,* are important Mahamudra texts. Stories of the eighty-four *mahasiddhas,* with their teaching and biographies, and another group of stories in the commentaries about thirty enlightened women, are sources of Mahamudra teachings.

The third source, the Menga, the oral instructions or transmission, derives from Lord Buddha and has continued all the way through all the masters of India, who brought it to Tibet, where it continued through the Tibetan masters. This is considered a very sacred part of the Mahamudra teaching, and before the oral transmission is received, much preparation is necessary.

The first phase of Mahamudra teaching is to listen, question, learn, and understand. Every question has an answer. The question itself is evidence that there is an answer, or it could not be asked. That is why asking questions after listening and thinking is so important. It helps us learn. To listen, question, and understand is the first instruction.

The second phase of Mahamudra has three steps. When something is understood intellectually, it is necessary to contemplate it. Intellectual apprehension can be sharp and satisfactory, but it can also be shallow. Most of the time intellectual understanding is quite shallow, although people might like to think they know all that is important to know. If most intellectual understanding went beyond the surface, the world today would not have so many problems caused by short-sightedness and lack of thinking about consequences. Contemplation deepens the understanding. Unexplored areas of the subject are examined, all ramifications are seen, and understanding becomes complete. This is extremely beneficial.

Once understanding is deepened through contemplation, confirmation comes. This deep assurance that you know, and know that you know, without question, is the result of contemplation. After confirmation, this understanding may be applied in daily life. No matter what a person may know or understand, this understanding is not going to do anything for development without application. The three stages of the second step are, then, contemplation, confirmation of understanding, and application of what is understood. Listen, learn, contemplate knowledge to understand it deeply, and then put it into action. When this is done, knowledge and understanding have great value and meaning.

These are the basic instructions. From here the Mahamudra practice becomes more specific, because it involves certain kinds of meditation. The Mahamudra meditation practices follow a threefold principle: the ground, the path, and the fruition.

There are many levels of understanding the ground, the path, and the fruition. Fundamentally, the ground is the cause and condition that provide a foundation for development. If we want to grow an orange tree, we must have fresh and healthy seeds. We plant them and care for the trees, and if everything goes well, we will have delicious oranges in a few years. In the case of sentient beings who wish to improve and attain enlightenment, there must similarly be a healthy cause and condition for them to do so. That is the most fundamental way to interpret the ground in Mahamudra.

If you see that somebody is not a good person now, and you wish that person to be better, you may want to teach that person to meditate, pray, or whatever, or at least explain and try to make the person understand how he or she can improve. Before doing this, you have to know that person has the ground for improvement, or your efforts will not succeed. It will be like trying to churn butter from water. There have to be causes and conditions for an evil sentient being to develop into a kind one. An example in Buddhist scripture is the robber and murderer Angulimala, who got his name from the string of human fingers he wore around his neck. He became a disciple of the Buddha, gave up his bad deeds, and became a great saint. We all know of contrary examples of people given many opportunities to improve who consistently fail to do so. They do not yet have the causes and conditions to take advantage of these opportunities.

From the Mahamudra point of view specifically, and from the Buddhist point of view generally, everything and everyone is perfect, ultimately. That is why even the worst being can become perfect if that being accumulates merit and purifies defilements. Then that being has the conditions for the seed, the essence of perfection within, to grow. That is the ground. It again brings us back to the beginning—every single sentient being has buddha nature. All phenomena are empty. Emptiness is the essence of all phenomena. Every sentient being's essence is buddha nature, emptiness, *dharmakaya*. Remember, according to the teaching of Lord Buddha, there is no ultimate negativity, weakness, or defilement. These are all relative things that are ultimately enlightenment.

Buddhists always pray that all sentient beings may be free from suffering and attain enlightenment. Because of the ground, this prayer, which may sound like an impossible dream, is realistic. If there were not this ground, the prayer would be a waste of time, a nice idea but entirely impractical. The foundation, all the bodhisattvic activity, all the Buddhist activity makes praying for the liberation of others valid and viable. Transport of a large amount of goods across a long distance from one point to another cannot be done by a horse alone, nor by a cart alone, nor by a driver alone. However, all three together can transport the goods. In the same way, understanding alone is not enough. Meditation alone is not enough. Activity alone is also not enough. All three must be put together for accomplishment to take place.

The path will go on until enlightenment. Whether it takes ten lifetimes or a million, the path goes all the way from the beginning of the practice until final enlightenment, the fruition. Until then, regardless of which level of ordinary being or bodhisattva you are, or what level of realization you reach, until full enlightenment, every single moment is the path. Although the different phases of development and realization might be described as levels of fruition, in terms of the Mahamudra definition of the ground, the path, and fruition, fruition refers only to the final fruition, buddhahood. The interim levels of realization, development, and fruition may be considered the path.

The path is the answer to the question of how to overcome relative obstacles. Our path is alive, it is not dead. It is not just history. It is an experience, a practice, an instruction—our path is alive. We certainly should be grateful for it. But it is also not the only path. If we think this path is the only path, we do not understand our path deeply enough. Doing anything perfectly, doing anything right, that is the path.

As Mahamudra practitioners, we sometimes have failure, sometimes have success, but we never give up. If our path follows Mahamudra instruction, we are told how to deal with anger, desire, jealousy, and pride—indeed, any kind of negative situation. Everyone knows what to do when they are hungry or thirsty. Through Mahamudra we learn how to meditate, which is the starting point of dealing with our negative thoughts, emotions, and life situations. We learn how to make some kind of sense of our ultimate nature and who we are. Of course, I know who I am when I see my photo. I recognize myself. But what am I behind this Tibetan face, this historical name of mine, and so forth? We must know ourselves beyond this name, face, and circumstance. Recognition of our fresh, purified, and enlightened natures, going beyond appearances, is the path.

The fruition can then be quite easy for us to see. The result, the destination, and the purpose of this path is the fruition. When we recognize what we are, that is the beginning of the fruition. But that's not really the fruition. The mere ability to recognize our true nature is not good enough. The realization of that recognition, that is enlightenment, the fruition.

Ground, path, and fruition are described in a text by one of the great masters of Mahamudra, the third Karmapa, Rangjung Rigpe Dorje. In his profound prayer he summed up the meaning and practice of Mahamudra. He said,

There is nothing to take away, and there is nothing to add.
When you look at the profound meaning profoundly,
You see the profound meaning profoundly.
Then you are liberated.

The path is limitless. It manifests according to the kind of relative obscurations, shortcomings, habits, or defilements that each of us has. The path is a remedy, a way through which we can deal with ourselves and with other human beings. The path is defined according to what is really there to work out, so it is impossible to talk about the path as a whole. It is individual and complex. We can talk about the available methods given in the teaching of the Buddha, which make the path something we can relate to. The direct words of the Buddha clarify our individual questions. It is a systematic method. The first thing we must have is a clear understanding of Buddha, his teaching, and how to follow his teaching. And after knowing that clearly and doing it, we may learn the methods and develop. There are many ways to go about it: by listening, questioning, contemplating, praying, meditating, doing good works.

When it comes to meditation, the first thing to develop is the ability to meditate effectively. All of us have the potential, but the ability has to be developed. The words of masters of the past can inspire our progress. Sometimes these words are meditative expression. They are definitely an important part of the instruction and transmission. In the four sentences quoted from the Mahamudra Prayer of the third Karmapa, the great master is talking about the mind, meditation, understanding, and liberation—Mahamudra. He is saying that everything is there, Buddha is within, there is nothing to take away, there is nothing to add. To get it right, you have to look at perfect truth perfectly and truthfully.

People often ask about attaining enlightenment in one lifetime. Theoretically speaking, of course one can attain enlightenment in one lifetime. It wouldn't even take one lifetime, it is just a moment, because buddha is within. Practically speaking, however, one life is not enough. If a disciple is able to perform with 50 percent of the total possible dedication and diligence, it might take two lifetimes. If the disciple is capable of exerting 100 percent commitment, it will take one lifetime. This is not usually possible. Many of us are in the minus-1 percent dedication category, so it will take us millions of lifetimes. The time it takes to become enlightened always depends on the effort and the dedication of the practitioner. Enlightenment itself wouldn't take one day. Like seeing the view from the top of a great mountain, it takes an instant to look and see it. Of course, it will have taken days or weeks of sweat and exertion, after years of preparation, to get to the place where you can see the view.

The next four sentences of the Mahamudra Prayer are about one of the important fundamental meditations of the Mahamudra teachings. They are about *shinay,* the meditation that develops calmness and clarity. It invokes the image of mind and the ocean. Thought and waves of the sea are used as metaphors. The four lines describe the benefit and also the state of the quiet mind, the mind at peace.

> *The rough and subtle thought, like the wave, is at peace.*
> *The motionless ocean of the mind is firmly at rest,*
> *Free of all stains of confusion and dullness.*
> *May the ocean of peace remain calm and unshaken.*

Now, this introduces a most important foundation for all meditation. If the mind is at peace, everything becomes simple. If the mind is not at peace, simple things become complicated. When something is complicated and confusing, naturally it takes a lot of time and effort to sort out the confusion, solve the problem, and start moving again. When there is no confusion, and things become clear, then every effort you make is directly beneficial and leads to improvement. You do not waste time and energy with confusion. This is an important fundamental step in meditation.

The four verses are about the second stage, after the development of the peaceful state of mind. The peaceful state of mind can be a relief, and it is very pleasant. The next stage is necessary to bring it from being just a peaceful state of mind, calm without too much further clarity, to a sharp and clear state of mind. This describes the importance of *lhatong*, insight or clarity, which is more than just a peaceful state of mind.

> *When looking at an object, there is no object.*
> *It is seen as mind.*
> *When looking at the mind, there is no mind.*
> *It is empty of existing essence.*

When looking at both, dualistic fixation is freed of itself.
May we realize the clear light, the nature of mind.

When you look at the mind that cannot be looked at, you see very clearly the meaning that cannot be seen. At that point, the doubt involving "This is" or "This is not" ceases completely. There is no doubt. One may recognize the unmistaken essence.

When you develop *shinay,* your mind is at peace. Then you observe that pure, peaceful mind. When you examine it, there will be no doubt about whether "this is" or "this is not." It isn't something that is different from you that you're seeing, as if it were another object, because you are seeing yourself, the essence of yourself. So that is the aspect of *lhatong* described by the third Karmapa.

The next four lines are about compassion. They introduce the definition of true or sacred compassion. Compassion has many levels, as we have seen, from ordinary caring to great loving-kindness. This is how the third Karmapa puts it:

The nature of every sentient being is Buddha,
But because they don't recognize it,
They circle in the sufferings of samsara.
May I develop pure compassion, Limitless One, towards all
sentient beings.

Now, the ordinary compassion that develops when you see somebody is in pain is very important, but that is quite different from the sacred, deep compassion, because the former can stem from personal ego. You may see somebody who is experiencing suffering while you are not suffering, and you have pity toward that person or being. It is not negative, but it is not complete compassion. Complete compassion comes when you know that the essence of this sentient being is not ignorance or suffering, that the essence of this sentient being is buddha. You know that because the sentient being does not recognize this, he or she is creating and experiencing suffering. Then your compassion is complete, with pure understanding, with respect, with compassion that is not condescension toward others who are suffering. It is compassion that flows from deep and clear understanding.

The superficial aspect of fruition is that every practice has its result. The first in the two stages of fruition comes because of this. If the first fruition is successfully dealt with by the practitioner, then the second fruition, enlightenment, will happen. The first one is called in Tibetan *nyam* and second *tokpa*.

The *nyam* phase happens first, and it is quite powerful. *Nyam* is the extraordinary signs and experiences that come before realization. Many practitioners who are without guidance of a good teacher, and who do not have proper understanding, might develop a great obstacle at this stage of fruition. *Nyam* is not an accomplishment; it is just a sign, an experience. In itself, it doesn't mean anything. It just means your practice is working, that's all. If a practitioner thinks *nyam* is accomplishment, he or she will get stuck there and go no further. And *nyam* can also become very harmful if one becomes attached to it, because when this happens a person might think he or she is enlightened, equal to the Lord Buddha or great bodhisattvas like Avalokiteshvara. But if the person is not enlightened, that is absolutely wrong. So when *nyam,* the first fruition, is experienced, the practitioner must be able to ignore it, not get excited about it. Do not become attached to the *nyam*. Great masters have given examples, saying that *nyam* is like a mist. It comes and it goes. So you don't hold on to it.

Tokpa is the actual realization, and that is enlightenment. That comes at the end; it is the final fruition. On the path to complete enlightenment, there are minor experiences of *nyam* and *tokpa*. According to whatever his or her practice is, the practitioner experiences the *nyam* of that practice, and later the *tokpa* of the accomplishment of that practice. This is one of the many reasons why a master teacher and also a lineage are very important in Buddhism. That is the only way you can be sure what *nyam* and *tokpa* and many other things experienced on the path really are.

It may be helpful to say a few words about the instructions that go with the practice, particularly how a beginner should practice. Beginners always get a little bit out of balance because they see the perfect quality of the practice and the Dharma in a very fresh and new way. It is a very inspiring and most personal thing. Encountering a valid and effective path to enlightenment is very precious indeed. But because of this specialness, the beginner usually overdoes things. Beginners should maintain their inspiration, devotion, and confidence, but they should be careful to maintain balance. Sometimes new practitioners burn out because they try to take on too much at once, and that is not beneficial. It is better to take up the practice with moderation and balance.

Beginners are normally physically and mentally tense. If someone is doing prostrations, he or she wants to do them as well and diligently as possible, and as much as possible. Or with prayer, a person may want to pray loudly and often. Beginners see the urgency, the impermanence, and all the confusion and defilements, so they really feel desperate, and this makes them tense. Of course, quantity has its importance, but quality is more important than quantity. So try to relax physically, try to relax mentally, and when you say a prayer, try also to say it with your heart—not just orally, loudly and often, but taking care to feel, know, and express the meaning while you say it. Life goes by very quickly. Impermanence is always there. There's urgency. But somehow it doesn't help to rush things, because there will not be real accomplishment. True understanding does not develop that way. You have to give it time.

It is like a child who tries to make a bonsai tree, and then becomes impatient and cuts away something every day or so. The tree will die. A bonsai takes decades of patient care and attention. Like a bonsai, you have to give yourself time and space to really develop. Mahamudra gives the practitioner all the space in the world, while at the same time incorporating every moment of living into the practice. It is through the small and simple things that we make the great gains later on: through contemplating the state of sentient beings, through simple *shinay* and *lhatong* meditation, through watching the breath. That is a powerful foundation for more specialized practices that will refine our knowledge and understanding of the Great Gesture which leads to enlightenment.

Free from mental creation, it is Mahamudra.
Free from extremes, it is the Great Middle Way.
Being all-inclusive, it is also called the Great Perfection.
May we gain certainty that by knowing one, all meanings
   are realized.

——— GLOSSARY ———

ABHIDHARMA (T: *chos-mngon-pa*) Literally, "realized truth." The term denotes the Buddhist system of knowledge, philosophy, and cosmology. It is one of the four divisions of the Vajrayana Buddhist canon: Vinaya, Sutra, Abhidharma, and Tantra.

ASANGA (T: *thogs-med-pa*) Buddhist teacher of the fourth century C.E. who transmitted essential teachings said to have been received from the bodhisattva Maitreya.

AVALOKITESHVARA (T: *spyan-ras-gzigs-dbang-phyug*) The bodhisattva of compassion, depicted holding the Wish-Fulfilling Gem between folded hands. The mantra associated with this bodhisattva is one of the most invoked by Tibetan Buddhists, OM MANI PADME HUNG.

BARDO (T: *bar-do*) The intermediate state between the end of one life and rebirth into another. Bardo also refers to the intermediate period between birth and death, and between sleeping and waking.

BHUMI (T: *sa*) Stage of attainment at the bodhisattva level of development. There are ten stages of achievement, after which complete enlightenment is possible.

BODHICHITTA (T: *byang-chub-kyi-sems*) Ultimate bodhichitta is the union of emptiness with compassion, beyond conceptualization. Relative bodhichitta is compassion characterized by the aspiration to liberate all sentient beings from suffering.

BODHISATTVA (T: *byang-chub-kyi-sems-dpa*) A future buddha; one who is committed to the practice of compassion and the six *paramitas,* or perfections.

BUDDHA (T: *sangs-rgyas*) An individual who attains, or the attainment of, complete enlightenment, such as the historical Shakyamuni Buddha.

BUDDHA NATURE (T: *sangs-rgyas-kyi-khams/rigs*) Unrealized enlightened mind, the essential nature of all sentient beings.

DEFILEMENTS. *See* Five Poisons or Defilements.

DHYANI BUDDHA (T: *rgyal-ba-rigs-lnga*) The completely purified state of the five elements and other components of sentient beings is embodied by five *dhyani* buddhas and their enlightened families. The five are Vairochana, Buddha family; Akshobhya, Vajra family; Ratnasambhava, Ratna family; Amitabha, Padma family; Amoghasiddhi, Karma family.

DUALISM (T: *gzung-dzingyi-lta-ba/gynis-snang*) Perception of duality that arises from ignorance and is present in all phenomena of cyclic existence; perception of subject and object, "I" and "other."

EMPTINESS (T: *stong-pa-nyid*) The doctrine that emptiness is the basis of everything, and that all concepts and phenomena are devoid of reality because they are the products of changeable conditions and therefore illusory. In Mahamudra practices, the play between emptiness and "reality" is used to realize emptiness, which is ultimately beginningless, ceaseless, and limitless.

ENLIGHTENMENT (T: *byang-chub*) The definition varies according to the Buddhist tradition. The Hinayana tradition defines enlightenment as the freedom from rebirth in samsara, with mind free of ignorance and emotional conflict. The Mahayana tradition holds that enlightenment is not complete without development of compassion and commitment to use skillful means to liberate all sentient beings. In the Vajrayana teachings, the foregoing stages of enlightenment are necessary, but ultimate enlightenment is a thorough purification of ego and concepts. The final fruition of complete liberation transcends all duality and conceptualization.

FIVE ELEMENTS (T: *byung-ba-lnga*) Earth, air, fire, water, and space are the five elements of the external world. They are manifested internally as five qualities: solid, fluid, heat, movement, and pressure (space).

FIVE POISONS OR DEFILEMENTS (T: *dug*) Temporary mental states that inhibit understanding: ignorance, pride, anger, desire, and jealousy. The three root poisons are ignorance, desire, and anger.

FOUR NOBLE TRUTHS (T: *phags-pai-ben-pa-bzhi*) The first teaching of Shakyamuni Buddha after his enlightenment, these are the doctrines that (1) life is suffering; (2) suffering has a cause; (3) suffering can cease; (4) there are means to eliminate suffering.

HINAYANA (T: *theg-pa-d,am-pa*) The first of three *yanas*, or vehicles, known as the "lesser vehicle." It includes in its teachings the path to the enlightenment of an *arhat*, one who is free of rebirth and who has transcended ignorance and conflicting emotions.

JENTONG (T: *gzhan stong*) A doctrine of emptiness based on the teachings of the Buddhist master Nagarjuna, *jentong* is the source of centuries of philosophical debate. In contrast to the *rangtong* view, which asserts all phenomena are intrinsically empty, the *jentong* view holds that all phenomena are not empty of their own nature or reality, but empty of conventional natures of dependence or conceptualization. It is called "other emptiness," a clear, nondual awareness. *See* Rangtong.

KAGYÜ (T: *bka-brgyud*) One of the four main traditions of Tibetan Buddhism, it is, as the name indicates, the lineage of oral transmission.

KAL NYUM (T: *kal-nyum*) "Equal timing"; refers to the karmic causes and conditions that result in all human beings experiencing phenomena in similar ways; the common ground of perception.

KANGYUR (T: *bka-gyur*) That part of the Tibetan Buddhist canon comprising the recorded teachings of the Buddha. The Tengyur, which consists of commentaries and practices, completes the canon.

KARMA (T: *las*) Action and the results of action. The actions of each sentient being are the causes that create the conditions of rebirth and the circumstances in that lifetime.

KARMAPA A lineage of incarnate bodhisattvas or *tülku*s in the Tibetan Buddhist Kagyu tradition. Karmapas are thought to be the incarnation of the bodhisattva Avalokiteshvara.

KAYAS, THREE These are the three bodies of a buddha: the *dharmakaya,* the enlightenment body of transcendent wisdom; the *sambhogakaya,* or enjoyment body, which is the means of compassionate communication with others; and the *nirmanakaya,* or emanation body, which is the physical form inhabited by a buddha when appearing in the human realm.

LHATONG (T: *lhag-mthong*) Vipashyana or insight meditation. These are analytical meditation techniques that develop insight into the actual nature of phenomena. Although mastery of *shinay,* or tranquility meditation, is usually recommended before beginning *lhatong,* some Vajrayana methods, like the Kagyü Mahamudra, utilize them together.

MAHAMUDRA (T: *phyag-rgya-chen-po*) The "great seal," the core meditation teaching of the Kagyü school of Tibetan Buddhism.

MAHAYANA (T: *theg-pa-chen-po*) The second of the three vehicles of Buddhism, called "the great vehicle." Mahayana schools of philosophy appeared several hundred years after the Buddha's death, although the tradition is traced to a teaching he is said to have given at Rajgriha, or Vulture Peak. The focus of Mahayana is development of compassion and the recognition of buddha nature in all sentient beings. In Mahayana, the purpose of enlightenment is to liberate all sentient beings from suffering as well as oneself.

MAITREYA (T: *byams-pa*) The name of the coming Buddha, who is said to dispense the Dharma as ruler of a celestial pure realm, Tushita heaven.

MANJUSHRI (T: *jam-dpal-bshes-gnyen*) The bodhisattva of wisdom and knowledge, depicted with a sword and a book.

OBSCURATIONS (T: *sgrib-pa*) There are two categories of obscurations: confused emotions and ignorance. The first category prevents sentient beings from freeing themselves from samsara, while the second prevents them from gaining accurate knowledge and realizing truth.

ORAL TRANSMISSION (T: *man-ngag*) A distinctive characteristic of Vajrayana Buddhism, in which meditation practices are conveyed from accomplished teacher to disciple in an unbroken lineage of transmission. Oral transmission of outer, inner, and secret teachings is essential for the student to be able to practice them.

PARAMITA (T: *pha-rol-tu-phyin-pa*) "Perfection" or perfect actions that help sentient beings transcend samsara. The six *paramitas* are: diligence, patience, morality, generosity, contemplation, and insight.

PHOWA (T: *pho-ba*) The transference of consciousness at the moment of death. This is a specific practice that must be learned prior to death, which enables an individual to eject the consciousness into a higher rebirth as the physical elements begin to dissolve at the time of death. An accomplished practitioner can facilitate the transference of consciousness for others also.

PURE LAND (T: *dag-zhing*) An environment that is completely free of suffering. It is the result of the pure and compassionate aspirations of a buddha. Birth in such a realm gives temporary respite from suffering and the opportunity to receive the teachings of the resident bodhisattva—for example, the Tushita heaven of the next buddha, Maitreya.

RANGTONG (T: *rang-stong*) The philosophical view that all phenomena are intrinsically empty, in contrast to the *jentong* view of "other emptiness," that phenomena are not intrinsically empty. *See* jentong.

REALMS OF EXISTENCE (T: *rigs-drug-gi-skye-gnas*) As a result of the twelve interdependent links and karma, sentient beings are reborn in six realms of existence: *deva*s, or celestial beings; *asura*s, or demigods, afflicted by jealousy; human beings, who experience all five defilements; animals, afflicted by ignorance; *preta*s, or hungry ghosts, afflicted by attachment and aversion; and hell-beings, afflicted by anger and hatred.

REINCARNATION Continuous, cyclic rebirth into the realm of samsara. Consciousness of an individual enters form according to his or her karma, the causes and conditions created by previous actions.

In the Buddhist view, ordinary beings reincarnate in one of six realms of existence, while those beings who have achieved the bodhisattva levels of enlightenment may incarnate in buddha-fields.

RELATIVE TRUTH   Describes the aspect of reality that is changeable, impermanent, and limited. It is a mundane manifestation of ultimate truth.

SAMSARA (T: *khor-ba*)   All the phenomena of existence arising out of ignorance and perpetuating the formation of karma, rebirth, and suffering.

SAMTEN (T: *bsam-gten*)   "Stable mind" or concentration. This is a meditative state important at the time of death. It involves a range of contemplative capabilities, including mindfulness, equanimity, neutral feeling, and single-pointed mind.

SENTIENT BEINGS (T: *sems-can*)   All beings with consciousness or mind who have not attained the liberation of buddhahood. This includes those individuals caught in the sufferings of samsara as well as those who have attained the levels of a bodhisattva.

SHINAY (T: *zhi-gnas*)   Calming of the mind through disciplined meditation practices that focus on internal processes such as the breath; tranquility meditation, also known as *samatha*.

SUTRA (T: *mdo*)   Texts in the Buddhist canon attributed directly to the Buddha. They are viewed as his recorded words, although they were not actually written down until many years after his *parinirvana*. They are usually in the form of dialogues between the Buddha and his disciples.

TANTRA (T: *rgyud*)   Literally, *tantra* means "continuity," and in Buddhism it refers to two specific things: the texts that describe the practices leading from ignorance to enlightenment, including commentaries by Tantric masters; and the way to enlightenment itself, encompassing the ground, path, and fruition.

TENGYUR (T: *bstan-gyur*)   That part of the Buddhist canon which comprises the instructions on the practices leading to liberation from suffering, and commentaries by Buddhist masters. The canon is completed by the Kangyur, the collection of Sutras, viewed as the actual recorded teachings of Shakyamuni Buddha.

TSA (T: *rtsa*)   *Nadi* in Sanskrit, this is an energy pathway in the subtle body, formed after conception of the physical body. The central channel is formed first, and from it develop branch channels to the left and right. The energy, or life force (*prana*), flows through these channels. These pathways are utilized in Buddhist meditation practices for the synchronization of body and mind.

TÜLKU (T: *sprul-sku*)   Tibetan word for *nirmanakaya* (*see* Kayas, three) denoting the "emanation body" of a buddha, according to classical texts. In Tibet, however, it came to mean the emanation body of an advanced Buddhist master who chooses to continue to incarnate for the benefit of others. The first such *tülku* to be recognized was the second Karmapa, Karma Pakshi, whose birth was predicted by his predecessor, the first Karmapa, Dusum Khyenpa.

TWELVE INTERDEPENDENT LINKS (T: *mdzad-pa-bcu-gyi-yan-lag-bcu-gnyis*)   Also known as dependent origination, this is the explanation given by the Buddha detailing the chain of causes and conditions that keep sentient beings bound in the wheel of rebirth. In Tibetan art it is depicted as a large wheel divided into twelve sections and held in the grasp of a giant demon.

ULTIMATE TRUTH   Truth beyond limitation or conceptualization; enlightened, pure truth unencumbered by change or duality.

VAJRAYANA (T: *rdorje-theg-pa*)   Literally, "diamondlike" or "indestructible vehicle," this third of the three vehicles of Buddhist teachings arose later than the Hinayana and Mahayana and consists largely of oral transmission of secret teachings. Literary evidence first appeared about 500 C.E., but it is likely the tradition existed much earlier, quietly passed on from master to disciple.

VINAYA (T: *dulba*)   Tenets of monastic discipline and ethics as presented in the Buddhist canon.

YANA (T: *theg-pa*)   A vehicle of Buddhist teaching. Tibetan Buddhism has three main vehicles: Hinayana, Mahayana, and Vajrayana.